THE ULTIMATE WORRY-FREE PREGNANCY GUIDE FOR DADS

9 SIMPLE STEPS TO CRACK THE DAD CODE, SUPPORT YOUR PARTNER AND BECOME A SUPER FIRST-TIME FATHER

CURTIS HOYLES

ABOUT THE AUTHOR

Curtis Hoyles was born on **December 1, 1987**, making him **thirty-four years old** in the summer of 2022. He grew up in a medium-sized town in the American Midwest.

He was part of the graduating class of 2010 from his local high school. He and his high school sweetheart, Linda, were already going steady at the time.

He went to college while his girlfriend worked as an independent artist selling art pieces and crafts on the then-new and upcoming Etsy. College life was hard for the young couple. Curtis had to work nights while studying during the day. They lived in a small apartment a few miles from the college and had to budget their money.

In May of 2010, Curtis graduated from college with a Business Degree (and a minor in English with the dream of becoming a Science Fiction novelist one day). He proposed to Linda soon after. They got married in the early fall of 2010.

Life got much easier for them after that. Curtis was immediately hired by a then-small startup, working in human resources and middle-management as the company grew fast. They were able to pay for Linda to start taking art classes at the local college, and they planned for her to get a full-on art degree one day, as her art pieces and crafts started selling really well online. A wrench was thrown into that marital bliss, however, when Linda found out she was pregnant in the summer of 2012.

Their first child, a boy named **Cody** was born on February 21, 2013. (This makes him nine years old, having just graduated from 3rd grade—and heading into 4th Grade—in the summer of 2022.)

A few years later, Linda turned out to be pregnant again. Their second child, a girl, was born on July 4, 2015. They named her **Liberty** because she was born on American Independence Day. (She'd be five and just about to start 1st Grade in the summer of 2022.)

Throughout the years, Curtis always dreamed of being the next George Lucas and writing the next Star Wars. He's got a massive word document on his hard drive—a novel he's never managed to finish. Then, during the COVID-19 pandemic, he started toying with writing a book about parenting. Having his kids at home and working from home during the pandemic made him think a lot about being a dad.

Finally, in the spring of 2022, as things opened up from the pandemic and the kids started going back to school, Curtis had a lot more time on his hands. He started writing in earnest on *The Dad Code*, with big plans to publish several books on being a dad.

CONTENTS

A FREE SURPRISE GIFT JUST FOR YOU!

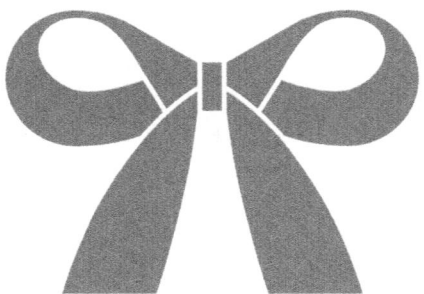

Thank you for purchasing my book.

For all my readers, I have a special thank-you gift that you can access by scanning the QR code below!

INTRODUCTION

"The guys who fear becoming fathers don't understand that fathering is not something perfect men do, but something that perfects the men."

— FRANK PITTMAN

The kid's face is turning purple, and everyone is staring.

You're in line at a comics and collectible store in your local mall. A guy near you, probably exactly your age or a little younger is red-faced and near panicking as he tries to corral his two young kids in the line behind you.

You're trying to be polite, so you don't turn around, but you can hear everything that's being said.

"Daddy, I want that!"

"No, don't touch it."

"Why not?"

"I said no."

"Why not?!"

Now, the oldest of the two kids, maybe four or five years old, is screaming and begging. The dad tries his best to keep the situation calm, but the younger of the two kids, maybe two, gets anxious and starts kicking and whining, yanking her hand away from her father's grasp.

You glance over your shoulder to see the four-year-old in a total fit, little hands in round, pudgy fists, face getting redder and redder, deepening to a raging violet. The dad glances around, embarrassed and lost, like the proverbial deer in the headlights. For a moment, his eyes meet yours, and you quickly turn back around, embarrassed for him.

Your heart goes out to the guy, especially when you hear him say under his breath, "Please! Don't do this now." But, at the same time, you breathe easy. As hard as things might get from time to time—with the job, bills and stress of both married life and homeowner-ship—at least you aren't that guy!

You're up next in line, and you're relieved to pay and get out of there before the tantrum gets worse. Poor dad. As you walk your way through the mall, you think about how hard his life must be, and how in over his head he seemed.

Kids are everywhere at the mall; from wailing newborns in strollers to toddlers with frantic moms or dads chasing after them to teenagers holding hands and making out in the food court. But nothing you observe on your way through the mall and out to your car is nearly as traumatic as the scene back in the collectibles shop.

You drive home to your house and expect to find your wife watching Netflix on the couch. But she's in bed, instead. What happened? Is she sick? Her stomach has been giving her trouble lately.

But when you ask her how she is, she can't speak. Instead, she hands you a long, plastic instrument. It takes you a moment to realize it's a pregnancy test. And on that test is something that will change your life forever.

Two red lines. Congratulations, bucko—you're going to be a father!

"I'M PREGNANT" – THE TWO SCARIEST WORDS IN THE ENGLISH LANGUAGE

Life comes at you fast, doesn't it?

Maybe you decided to grab adult life by the horns—work, family, a home, and car, grown-up friends and hobbies—and it's been a blast, but it's also a bit overwhelming at times.

There never seems to be enough time. Work drains you, but you know putting in that overtime and going the extra mile will get you places later on in your career. Or maybe you've been developing a side hustle in the evenings and weekends, hoping to quit the day job and chase your dream before you're too old and full of regrets. Then there's family life. Getting married (or moving in with your partner) was a huge and magical step, but the couple's life brings with it new adult responsibilities. Now you're making decisions like you remember your parents doing when you were a kid—you're discussing the pros and cons of where to live or what to do on the weekends. Married life becomes a vortex that eats up more of your time. And then, of course, you need time to relax, too, right?

Money is another thing there never seems to be enough of. Between bills, taxes and parking tickets, subscription services, and food deliveries, you feel like every time you turn around, you're having to pay for yet another aspect of that grownup life you dreamed of as a kid.

Hopefully, after a couple of years of all of these commitments, you start to feel like you've got things figured out . . . at least just a little bit. It's like playing a video game, and you've finally gotten the hang of all the controls. I remember that feeling myself, finally realizing that adult life isn't all that bad. Sure, you have plenty of responsibilities, but there are also lots of rewards. And finally finding that *special someone* to spend your life with makes everything simultaneously more challenging and more wonderful. All the hard work, budgeting, and getting up early? Well, maybe it's not that bad, after all.

Then something happens that throws a wrench into the nice groove you've settled into. If it's happened to you as it happened to me, it came at the most unexpected of times, and it's something that, once it's happened, there isn't anything you can do to undo it.

That positive pregnancy test . . .

Don't get me wrong. Fatherhood is a blast, and everything I said above about married or couple life—about how it's rewarding and worth all the extra effort and responsibility—applies doubly to parenthood. But that doesn't mean finding out you're expecting isn't one of the scariest scenarios a guy can go through. After all, it's one of the biggest changes in anyone's life.

Not to mention the level of responsibility! Think about it this way . . .

If you screw up at work—and I mean really bad—what's the worst that can happen? Well, unless you did something illegal and could go to jail—and let's assume you didn't screw up *that* bad—then the worst that could happen is you lose your job, right? That might be a scary thought, but you also know it's not the end of the world. After all, people change jobs all the time.

If you skip a few payments on your car or house, that would be pretty bad, too. But it's not the end of the world. There are plenty of financial help institutions out there that can help you get debts under control, even if it means a lot of cutting back.

Basically, all of the big responsibilities in your life come with some pretty nasty consequences if you drop the ball. But none of those consequences are earth-shattering. You might mess up at some point, but you'll bounce back.

But what about fatherhood? Now, that's a responsibility that carries along with it some major consequences! You might be looking at that positive pregnancy test your wife or partner just showed you and might be thinking: *What if I mess this up? I'd be messing up this child's life! That's serious business.*

And, indeed, it is. Even if you were planning on having kids, and the pregnancy came at exactly the right time because you were trying to conceive and have been preparing for a baby to enter your life, even then the realization that this is really happening—that you'll soon be responsible for a tiny human being for the next 18-plus years—might be a sobering thought.

THE UNPREPARED DAD

There are literally hundreds of books, video series, pamphlets, classes, podcasts, and mobile apps dedicated to coaching expecting mothers through their pregnancy. There's even a medical specialization dedicated to helping pregnant women have healthy babies.

It's wonderful that mothers get so much help and support—they definitely need it—but what about fathers?

All too often, the dad is pushed out of the picture. The running joke, immortalized by sitcoms and stand-up comedians, is that after conception (a.k.a. "the fun part"), a father's job is essentially done. Who needs him anymore? Now it's all about the mother and her relationship with her body and her child. Dad's just along for the ride.

Well, let me tell you it certainly doesn't have to be that way. In fact, I firmly believe it *shouldn't* be that way at all. As a father, your job doesn't *end* with conception; it *begins* at conception.

Your job as a father isn't just about getting out of the way and letting your partner take it from here. It's about being supportive and cooperative. It's about the two of you, mother and father, working together to bring a child into this world and raise that child to the best of your abilities.

If that concept appeals to you, then you're reading the right book, because I'm going to show you exactly how to make a success of fatherhood. But first, why is being a father so scary? We've already talked about the great responsibility involved. But there's another great disadvantage many first-time dads have to contend with—a total lack of preparation and instruction.

As I mentioned above, mothers get all kinds of support from books, videos, online and in-person courses—you name it. But the amount of material out there for first-time dads is ridiculously scarce.

That's exactly why I felt compelled to write this book. I wanted to include all the things I wish I knew when I had my first kid. Before I get into what this book is designed to teach you, let me tell you a bit about who I am. After all, I want you to have the confidence and trust that I know what I'm talking about. Let me tell you my story.

MY FATHERHOOD STORY

My name is Curtis, who you probably already know because my name is on the cover of this book. But what the cover doesn't tell you is that I was completely blind-sided when my wife informed me she was pregnant. It's worse than that, really, because I was in denial. I forced my wife to take two more tests and go to a doctor before I allowed myself to believe this was happening—we were going to have a baby.

Don't get me wrong; kids were always in the plan. But they were a "someday maybe" kind of thing for us. My wife had a great job working from home, and I was in the human resource department of a startup that was growing fast and doing cool stuff. You might think, *Human resources? What a drag!* But if you're a people person like me, then the job isn't all that bad at all. Plus, I had a side thing going—a mind-bending sci-fi novel I always dreamed would make me the next George Lucas.

Then the pregnancy happened, and we were totally not ready. My wife—because she's awesome and better than me in so many ways—adapted to the prospect of motherhood with the grace and confidence of an Olympic figure skater on ice. But I was scared out of my mind, and I'm not afraid to admit it.

So what did I do? I jumped on YouTube and spent an entire weekend watching every video with the word "father" in the title. By Sunday night, I was red-eyed, tired, and not much better prepared than when I started. So, the next day after work, I hit the library and read every book on parenting I could get my hands on.

I wish I could tell you I found the secret answer along the way. It wasn't that easy. But I'm a determined guy, so I kept searching, learning, and studying. It kind of became an obsession for me. I was determined to be the best dad I could be.

Along the way, I had an awesome circle of friends that were years ahead of me in their fatherhood journeys.

They gave me invaluable advice—through pregnancy and after the baby was born, through all the big steps of diaper changing to my child's first steps to the first day of school.

And now? Well, my oldest just turned nine and my second is in kindergarten. I'm the father of two kids, and they are everything to me. I'm not going to lie and say I did everything right—and I'm sure I still have plenty of mistakes to make along the way. But I really feel like the combination of relentless research and life experience brought me to where I am now.

This book is my gift to you, especially if you just found out your wife or partner is pregnant and you're as driven as I was to be the guy that actually deserves the cheesy "World's Greatest Dad" coffee mug someone's going to gift you for Father's Day at some point.

The word "Code" is in the title of this book, so you might be wondering: *Your story's nice and all, but what's the code?*

Well, I'm going to tell you right now, up front.

THE DAD CODE IN FOUR LETTERS: P-A-R-R

Let me get one thing out there right now. You may be nervous about having a kid, and that's normal. You may be feeling a lot of pressure to get things right, to be perfect. I know, I did. (Thus my hundreds of hours watching videos and reading dense books by psychologists and doctors.)

But you don't have to be perfect to be an amazing dad. You'll make mistakes along the way, and that's okay. Lord knows I made my share of mistakes, and my kids are turning out just fine.

This whole thing is scary. So let yourself be scared. Anxiety in itself isn't a bad thing because it moves us to take positive action. Reading this book is positive action (so congratulations!). But throughout the chapters to follow, there will be action points for you to apply, both during pregnancy and during your baby's first months.

This book is designed to equip you with the bare-bones, most crucial stuff I wish I'd known from the first moment my wife showed me a pregnancy test with those two red lines glaring at me. And everything can be summed up in four letters: P-A-R-R.

That's right! P-A-R-R. Did you ever see that animated movie *The Incredibles*? If not, go watch it. It's fairly entertaining. But the father's name in that movie is Bob Parr. P-A-R-R, Parr. That will help you remember.

We're going to be talking about P-A-R-R throughout the book. It applies to every chapter for the rest of the book, so it's a good idea to get a handle on it now. So what does P-A-R-R stand for?

The P stands for **Partner**. As we said above, dads are sometimes shoved aside once the wife is pregnant. But I firmly believe that a good father is a good partner to his wife or significant other throughout the pregnancy and beyond. The biological truth is the mother's body will be doing all the hard work for nine months straight, but a stellar father is there to support her and help her with her physical, mental, and emotional needs. A healthy mother, after all, typically results in a healthy baby.

The A stands for **Age**. It's a reminder that a mother's job dramatically changes depending on the child's age, and so do a father's responsibilities. Dads have to be responsive and dynamic in providing for both the mother and the baby. Your obligations will change as the newborn grows, and you'll have to get used to that constant change.

The R's both stand for **Relationship**. There are two of them to remind you that you have to cultivate, grow, and nurture a positive relationship with two people in your life now: your wife or partner and your baby. Both these relationships are important even during pregnancy. In this book, I'll show you how to create and maintain a strong bond with your baby—something traditionalists say only happens between mother and child.

If you want to summarize the Dad Code in the simplest possible way, just think P-A-R-R, and you'll be there most of the way. Throughout this book, we'll apply this code to the pregnancy, birth, and newborn stages of parenthood.

WHAT TO EXPECT IN THIS BOOK

Obviously, we'll be talking a lot about the above code, P-A-R-R, and how you can apply it throughout your wife's pregnancy and the baby's first few months. But I want to give you a bit of a roadmap with a few highlights of things to look forward to.

So, in this book, we'll cover topics such as:

- What you should expect when your wife is pregnant
- The #1 thing your wife needs from you during pregnancy—and how you can do it right
- Why your partner should exercise during pregnancy—and what exercises to try and avoid
- The signs that your baby is coming soon . . . and how you can prepare for it

- What to say and not to say to your partner after she gives birth (don't pay attention to these, and you'll ruin your relationship)
- How to decide whether to breastfeed or formula feed your newborn
- How to help your newborn start to develop a circadian rhythm
- How to strengthen both your relationship with your newborn and with your partner after delivery

Each of the above points will include the Dad Code, P-A-R-R, and plenty of my own experiences along the way.

So strap in, and let's get cracking—I mean coding!

To get things started, let's talk about what you should expect when your wife is expecting. If you haven't figured it out already, pregnancy will mean huge changes for you and her. What are some of those changes, and how can you apply P-A-R-R to help your wife or partner through them? The following chapter will dive into just that.

1

EXPECT SIGNIFICANT CHANGES

O kay, confession time.

That little scene I described at the start of this book's introduction wasn't a fun bit of fiction I dreamed up to grab your attention. It actually happened. And it happened to me.

I was the guy in the collectibles shop, trying to ignore the young father and his two kids behind me. And, while seeing his lost and embarrassed expression did scare me, I walked out of that mall thinking, *Man, I'm glad I'm not that guy!*

Then I came home and found out my wife was pregnant!

I immediately jumped into the five stages of grief, starting with denial. As I said before, I made my wife repeat the pregnancy test and go to a doctor before I'd finally accept the fact that we were expecting.

But from that first moment my wife, Linda, showed me that positive pregnancy test, and with that scene in the mall still fresh on my mind, deep down inside, I knew one thing in the depths of my soul: *My life was going to change forever.*

Of course, my mind went to the same place your mind probably did when your wife or partner told you she was pregnant. I immediately started thinking about all the changes a baby would bring into my life.

The first thing I started worrying about was money. We'd only been married a couple of years, and I was the only one in the family with a full-time job. Thankfully, the company I work for has always paid me fairly, but that paycheck would usually disappear pretty quickly. We had a house and a car payment to worry about, plus all the standard utilities and bills. I was making ends meet, but sometimes just barely.

Linda is an amazing artist. She paints incredibly beautiful stuff on canvases, but she really likes painting on small items like seashells, rocks, and other small things. She turned that skill into something profitable by selling custom art items and handmade jewelry. She'd managed to sell a few pieces a month on platforms like Etsy. It was a small business, but I was proud of her, even though, starting out, she usually barely made enough to pay for the paints she'd used to make the item she was selling.

So, even with both of us working, I at an office and Linda from home, we weren't exactly rolling in extra cash. Most months, we made ends meet with just enough to get a pizza on the weekends or something.

So, yeah, the thought of a baby definitely made me nervous. And financial issues were just the first in a long line of challenges I envisioned would come along with taking care of a child. But, do you know what? While I was already looking ahead to fatherhood, to having the baby here with us, there was another major challenge I wasn't even thinking about until it practically slapped me in the face: *The pregnancy itself!*

STRAP IN FOR A CRAZY NINE MONTHS

Changes can be scary, but they can also be good. By the time you reach adulthood, you're probably already familiar with rocky but ultimately positive changes in your life. Going from elementary school to middle school—then from middle school to high school—was a momentous change, right? Maybe it was even a bit scary for you. (I was terrified of starting high school, personally. And don't even get me started about college.) But those changes led to bigger and better things in life, right?

Going from school life to adult working life is a huge change, too. I had to work my way through college, Linda and I living in a tiny apartment within walking distance from my school so I wouldn't have to pay for transportation every day. But going from working nights as a student to taking on a full-time position at a small but growing tech company was a huge change for me.

Each change in life is kind of like walking through a doorway, going from one "room" of your life to a completely new place.

That's what life is, right? It's a series of changes. But pregnancy, I came to realize, was a double change. It's not a doorway. It's an elevator—you get on the elevator as a couple and get off at the top floor as a family with a baby. That nine-month elevator ride is a rocky transition period with its own set of changes and challenges that you and your partner are going to need to face together.

That's right; I said *together*. I want you to switch out the thought of "she's pregnant" and change it to "we're pregnant." Because getting through pregnancy absolutely should be a team effort!

A lot of people think of pregnancy as something the mother goes through alone. How many guidebooks are out there to help first-time mothers get through those nine months of great physical and emotional change? But plenty of people (including pregnant mothers or their partners, sometimes) completely fail to think about what the father goes through during this time, as well as what he can do to support his pregnant partner. The truth is, pregnancy brings a lot of changes for both partners involved, and it's helpful to know about these changes going in, so you can be prepared.

So let's talk about some of the changes you can expect while you're expecting. After all, the Dad Code (remember P-A-R-R?) absolutely applies throughout pregnancy as well as after the baby is born. I've divided these challenges into three main categories. So, let's start with the first category, which involves a shift in focus from you to *her*.

A SHIFT IN FOCUS

I go to work and make my way to my office. I'm not Mr. Popular at work or anything like that, but I have plenty of friends there. I'm a likable guy; what can I say?

Every workmate I pass on the way to my desk looks up and greets me. I'm used to things like "Hey Curt!" or "How are you?" But now that my wife is expecting, nobody seems to care about me. Instead, every person I meet has the same question: "How's Linda? How's your pregnant wife?"

Even my mom jumps on board. I get at least three text messages a day, and none of them are asking about me or my day. "How's the pregnant missy doing?" my mom asks constantly.

This is what I mean by a shift in focus. When you're a couple, you both get equal attention. When your relationship is new, and the romance is still fresh and exciting, you shower each other with attention. Your friends want to know how you are or what you're up to. If your friends are constantly asking about your wife, you might start to get suspicious, right? It's weird. But all that changes the second the world finds out she's pregnant.

Suddenly, she's going to be getting a lot more attention. For nine whole months, it will seem that the whole world has almost forgotten about you, the guy, as everyone is only focused on your partner and the little human growing inside of her.

Some guys I've talked to start to feel a bit left out during the pregnancy. Based on what I've read, this is natural. It doesn't mean you're a bad person or a selfish person. It just takes some getting used to. In fact, I say you should embrace the shift in focus because, after the baby is born, nothing will be the same again.

Your child will now be a major part of your life, which applies to you and your wife or partner. You'll both be paying a lot more attention to the baby and less attention to each other. It doesn't mean you don't love each other anymore or that romance is a thing of the past. It's just the way things are.

Along this long and strange elevator ride to parenthood, you'll need to expect a lot more doctor's appointments. During both of my wife's pregnancies, the doctors suggested she avoid driving at a certain point, which meant I was the official chauffeur to all her appointments. And sometimes, it felt like we were going to two or three appointments weekly! I swear I'd never been to a doctor so many times in my entire life.

Pregnancy is a huge ordeal for your partner's body, so she'll need the extra medical support.

In addition to going to the doctor, the two of you may start attending birthing classes. This is a great option, especially for first-time parents. Not only do these classes help you both prepare for the big day, but they also put you in contact with other couples going through the same process. Linda and I made some great friends at those birthing classes we attended, and we've kept in touch all this time, even though it's been nearly a decade since we were expecting our first child.

If you choose to go to some sort of class, be sure to take it seriously. Listen carefully and ask questions—no matter how dumb they sound in your head. Your wife or partner needs to see that you're supporting the pregnancy. Remember that the double-R in P-A-R-R stands for the relationships you'll have with both your partner and your baby. These classes are a wonderful way to strengthen your relationship as a couple during pregnancy.

Some places even offer exclusive fatherhood classes and clubs. Why not try one out to see if it's for you?

This whole shift in focus—both in the attention people pay to you as a couple and to what now fills your schedule—can be a bit jarring for some expecting fathers. But embracing the change and facing it head-on will be better for you than rejecting it, even if it means less time for video games, other hobbies, or spending time with your non-daddy friends.

HER UPS AND DOWNS

To say that pregnancy is a major change for a woman's body would be the understatement of the century. From the moment she becomes pregnant, after all, your partner is no longer one person. She's two, which means huge hormonal shifts, mental and emotional makeup, and physicality. When my wife was pregnant with our first—I think about five months into the pregnancy—I actually accused her of being a completely different person than the woman I married. Yeah, I probably should have put it more gently, but that was how I felt at the time. Maybe if I'd been warned about some of the biggest changes she would experience, I wouldn't have reacted that way.

So, it's best to expect the following changes in your pregnant partner. Keep in mind that each woman and pregnancy are different, so some of these things may not apply at all while others may apply doubly. But it's best to be prepared for anything, right?

Morning sickness. More than half of pregnant women report feeling some level of morning sickness early on in the pregnancy. It might be tough to see your loved one going through the daily rounds of nausea, especially when you know there isn't much you can do to make her feel better. Try keeping some saltine crackers and soda on hand to help calm her stomach when the morning sickness strikes.

Sensitive nose and strange cravings. Hollywood loves to show pregnant women with wacky cravings for odd food combinations—and this is definitely grounded in reality. Expect to be sent to the store (or using a delivery service app, thanks to the miracle of modern technology) for the strangest foods at the strangest times. Also, expect your partner's sense of smell and taste to become both very sensitive and sometimes out of whack. During our second pregnancy, we weren't allowed to have any chicken—raw, cooked, or packaged —in the house for over a month because my wife could smell it a mile away, and the scent would turn her stomach. (Did I sneak out for some Chick-fil-A during the pregnancy? Sure I did. What can I say? I'm only human. But I'd make sure to brush my teeth or chew some seriously strong gum before getting home so Linda wouldn't smell it and get nauseous.)

Sleeping more. Growing a baby inside of you is hard work, and that means your partner will experience days of complete exhaustion. The best thing she can do when her energy levels are low is to rest more than usual. This also means she may want to go to bed earlier or sleep in. Be sure to let her! Of course, that means you can catch up on sleep, too, or binging that show on Netflix you two have meant to catch up on. Relaxing together is a great way to stay connected during the pregnancy. (Remember that second R in P-A-R-R!) But your partner needs to come first during this time. So if you can get up and handle some things around the house so she can sleep or rest a bit more, you'll be helping her body focus on its primary job during the pregnancy—growing a healthy baby!

Swings in sex drive. Some couples report less intimacy during their pregnancy. But others report more. Each pregnant woman is different, and her sex drive could shift dramatically from one day to another. As her belly swells, some sexual positions may not be comfortable for her anymore. It's best to openly and honestly communicate during times of intimacy. And if either of you has any concerns, don't be bashful about talking to her doctor. (They get more questions about sex than you'd believe.)

Her mood swings. The other part of pregnancy that Hollywood often gets right has to do with sudden mood swings. Being pregnant is tough on the body, mind, and soul. It involves massive changes in hormones. On top of that, it can be a surprising and scary experience for the one carrying the child! One moment, it feels magical, and the next, it's terrifying. Your partner may become suddenly insecure, worried about being a bad mother, or self-conscious about the size of her belly. You may sometimes feel overwhelmed by these sudden mood swings but remember this: those swings are scary for her, too. Deal with them together. Be patient and listen to her express herself. Make her feel beautiful.

As an extra note, it's also not fair to blame every mood swing or moment of irritability on hormones because that doesn't dignify your partner either. Sure, hormones are responsible for plenty during pregnancy, but your wife will also have good reason to be upset, happy, angry, or scared at times. Returning to the above point, pregnancy is tiring. When we're tired, we tend to get grumpy or irritable, right? The same is true when we're physically uncomfortable, and discomfort is a constant experience during pregnancy. So dignify your partner by refraining from always blaming the hormones. Instead, be communicative. Learn to be a good listener. Just be there for her, but also be okay with giving her some space when she asks for it.

CONSTANT EXPECTATION

Let's get back to the analogy of the elevator. Pregnancy is like getting on a long elevator ride—perhaps to the top floor of the tallest building in town. What's waiting for you at the top? Imagine it's something big and scary, like a job interview that could change your life forever.

As the elevator slowly climbs—too slowly—you start to think, and the numbers on the display panel slowly count up, with your heart thudding. You have more butterflies in your stomach than in the entire Amazonian rain forest. And you may start to think the anticipation will kill you before you ever get there!

In much the same way, pregnancy can feel like that elevator ride. Sometimes it will feel like those nine months are just racing by because of all the changes coming at you in rapid-fire style. But, at other times, you may feel like time is ticking by at a snail's pace. This is because of the constant anticipation.

You'll spend a lot of time planning for the baby, preparing a crib, diapers, toys, and clothes. You'll spend hours looking at baby name lists (or debating which names to choose). As the pregnancy nears its end, the doctor's visits will become more frequent, and you'll be preparing for labor.

You may even have false alarms. Some women go into false labor multiple times before the real thing. That can be exciting—and an excellent opportunity to make sure you are truly prepared—but it can also be tiring. For some reason, almost every false labor Linda experienced was in the middle of the night, which is a truly exhausting experience.

The constant sense of anticipation can be stressful and exhausting for both of you. But remember that it's something that will pass. Before you know it, the pregnancy will be over, and the baby will be there!

FACE THE CHANGE AS A TEAM

It takes two to tango. You've heard that expression before, right? While it's often considered a given that your baby was conceived only through the coordinated efforts of both of you, the nine-month period of pregnancy is not always seen as a time of teamwork.

Movies often make this false impression worse. Men are often shown as basically enduring their wife or partner's pregnancy. But this exciting time is not something to be endured; it's something to be faced together, a collection of changes and challenges both of you can meet head-on. Remember, the P of the Dad Code stands for "partner." So you absolutely must face pregnancy as partners. That way, your whole family will thrive.

Get on that elevator together! Be there for your partner as much as humanly possible. Support her through every change and weather the storms of anticipation, anxiety, and excitement together.

If you do so, you'll find that the process of growing a baby will actually bring the two of you closer together. It will prepare both of you for the new and exciting challenges of parenthood to come!

So far, we've seen a bit about what to expect during your partner's pregnancy. But we've only scratched the surface on how you can help her through this time. In the following chapters, I want to teach you how to be that supportive team member your partner needs and deserves.

2

SUPPORT HER DURING PREGNANCY

I t was two in the morning. I was dead asleep, and I mean a level of sleep, dreaming of piloting an X-wing alongside Luke Skywalker. Suddenly my nerd dream is disturbed by a high-pitched noise.

I jump up in bed, looking around, yelling, "What's wrong?" in a groggy voice, just in time to see my wife rushing to the bathroom. She starts throwing up.

This is the second time this week. The doctor said she'd deal with nausea for a while, but this is ridiculous. A few minutes later, she's cleaning up and brushing her teeth, and the pillow is calling me back to sleepy land.

I have a difficult decision to make. I could lay back and drift away, or I could get up and see if Linda needs anything. I start running the pros and cons in my head, but I'm just too tired to think straight! Plus, I have a big report due tomorrow at the office.

After stalling as long as I can, I drag myself out of bed and offer to get Linda a glass of water or something. The look she gives me is both apologetic and thankful. She knows I'm tired. I don't have to rub it in. But I can tell she doesn't want to be alone.

So, we stay up for a while and watch an episode of her favorite show, which we had on DVDs back then before Netflix was a thing.

Now, that happened during our first pregnancy, a couple of months after we found out Linda was expecting. Was I a little extra tired the next day at work? Sure. But that pales in comparison with the support I was able to give Linda.

Essentially, that's what this chapter is all about—support. It's about being there for your wife or partner during the pregnancy, giving them the emotional support they need. But why is emotional support so important? Let's talk about three huge reasons, and then we'll talk about how you can give that much-needed support.

PREGNANCY IS SCARY

As already discussed in the preceding chapter, pregnancy is a rocky time full of challenges and major changes. But one thing we barely touched on was how scary being pregnant could be for your wife.

Your wife or partner is experiencing changes to her body that she doesn't understand. Everyday things can become uncomfortable or painful. Her body is changing and growing, and her hormones are constantly shifting.

On top of all that is the responsibility that comes with carrying a baby around in your womb. As a dad, you'll never have to worry about being responsible for a tiny living creature every hour of the day. By the time you interact directly with your child, they'll be a baby you can pick up, put down, or pass off to someone else to take care of. But during pregnancy, your wife doesn't have any of those options.

Every decision your wife makes, day and night, could affect the baby. That level of responsibility can be very stressful.

Another stressful and scary part of pregnancy is the thought of anything going wrong during pregnancy or labor. As a dad, you've probably already started worrying about that, too. I remember having recurring nightmares of something going wrong in the delivery room when Linda was pregnant with our second child, Liberty.

But whatever worries you harbor are nothing compared to the fears your partner will be going through!

That said, you don't want your wife to face all of that fear and anxiety on her own, do you? When you give her the support she needs, you're essentially telling her that you're going to be right there with her—every step of the way!

The P in P-A-R-R stands for "partners," remember? So show your wife through your words and actions that you're facing pregnancy and parenthood as partners, and you'll bring her a lot of much-needed relief.

HAPPY EQUALS HEALTHY

A second reason to give your wife or partner support is that keeping her happy will go a long way to keeping her healthy. Leaving her with the stress, on the other hand, will only put her—and the baby—in even more danger.

You've probably heard that stress is a silent killer, right? The second I turned thirty, my doctor started badgering me about my stress levels, as well as my blood pressure and cholesterol. He told me, under no uncertain terms, that living an unnecessarily stressful life would shave years, or even decades, off my lifespan. Of course, as a father of two trying to make ends meet, I do the best I can to manage stress, but those same principles apply to your wife or partner during pregnancy.

We'll talk more later about how you can directly help with your wife's health while she's expecting. But, for now, keep in mind that keeping your wife happy and relatively stress-free—by supporting her during the pregnancy—is a great way to boost both her health and the health of your unborn baby.

THE DOUBLE-R OF THE DAD CODE

As a third reason for supporting your wife throughout the pregnancy, remember the double-R in the Dad Code, P-A-R-R. Those two R's represent your double relationship with your partner and with your baby.

While there are some things you can do to start building a relationship with your child while it's in the womb—and we'll get into some of that later in this book—the pregnancy is your last opportunity to focus all of your energies on strengthening your relationship with your partner.

After the baby is born, you'll no longer be a couple. Your lives will change completely, and many of the things you used to be able to do together will no longer be an option (or will get much harder to plan). A simple romantic evening out is something you can do on a whim now, but once the baby is born, you'll have to arrange for a sitter and plan out your dates, at least for a few years.

So, while you still have that freedom and couple dynamic, showing as much support for your pregnant wife or partner now is the perfect way to strengthen your relationship as a couple. That will, in turn, enable you to face the challenges of parenthood as a united team.

Think of it as strengthening your castle walls before a siege. I'm not insinuating the baby is an invader or anything, but you get the idea!

So, now that we have secured in our minds why providing that emotional support during pregnancy is so important, what are some ways you can take action? Let's look at a few together. Actually, I've put together quite the list, so let's get started!

#1: BE AN INFORMED DADDY

I've told you how I became obsessed with learning everything I could about parenthood, fatherhood, pregnancy, and child-rearing when my wife was pregnant with our first child. I read every book in our local library about having children and visited every website, blog, and email newsletter Google would tell me about. I became obsessed with information.

I didn't realize it until much later, like a year after our son was born, but Linda felt a great sense of relief because I was taking fatherhood so seriously. I wasn't doing it for that reason, mind you. But it turned out that being informed and doing my research was a great way to show my support.

You're already doing that just by reading this book. But you can do even more to show your partner this is serious for you. You can take birthing classes with her or even fatherhood classes on your own. You can read up on the biology of pregnancy.

The more you know, the better prepared you'll be to support your wife in all kinds of ways. My advice is to take a couple of hours every week to do some extra research on pregnancy and child-rearing. You'll be surprised by what you learn!

#2: LEARN TO BE HELPFUL

Pregnancy will take its toll on your wife's energy levels. She's going to need more sleep than before, and she'll need to rest more often. That means you have an excellent opportunity to be more supportive around the house.

Be on the lookout for ways you can help her out. The best thing you can do is find ways to do things for her without her having to ask you. That way, you're supporting her physically by allowing her to rest more, but you're also supporting her emotionally because you're showing yourself to be attentive to her needs.

So why not take on a few extra chores around the house? Before our first kid, I wasn't exactly the kind of guy you wanted messing around in the kitchen. I could grill stuff, sure, but that was outside, flipping burgers and drinking beers. You know, the man stuff! During Linda's pregnancy, I learned to cook quite a few meals in the kitchen. A few times, I even surprised her with some amazing dishes she'd had no idea I could make. Thanks, YouTube!

Another big part of being supportive and helpful is in adjusting to her new needs. For example, many pregnant women benefit from buying and sleeping with a full-body or pregnancy pillow. These extra-large pillows are often specifically shaped to provide a pregnant woman with extra support and comfort while sleeping—especially later in the pregnancy when that large belly can become a constant discomfort. You can be helpful by proactively helping her select a pillow. And you can be supportive by adjusting to the limited space you'll have left in the bed to accommodate the large pillow.

#3: SUPPORT HER LIFESTYLE CHANGES

Your wife's doctor may put her on a special diet during the pregnancy. Even if not, while you're doing your research (remember what I mentioned above?), you may find some good tips on nutrition to help your wife stay healthy while expecting.

Of course, if your partner drinks or smokes, those things will also have to be cut out throughout the pregnancy.

How can you support your wife through that time? Why not try to make the same lifestyle changes she has to make? A better diet will anyway help stave off that dreaded "dad bod." Plus, you'll be able to support her through some difficult changes in her eating habits.

Of course, when it comes to smoking, I don't have to be a doctor to tell you that it's a horrible habit. If your wife is quitting, you really should, too. Second-hand smoke is super dangerous, both for your partner and for the baby. Plus, you'll live longer, so that's a big bonus!

#4: BECOME A GOOD LISTENER

This isn't rocket science. If you want to support your wife emotionally, being a good listener is a huge part of that. Learn to listen patiently as she talks about her fears or describes what's happening with her body. Be sincerely interested!

I'll tell you a secret about good listening: the more you do it, the better you get at it and the more into it you'll be. It's kind of like drinking water. If all you drink is soda or beer all day long, then a glass of plain water may taste nasty to you. But the more you drink water, a little every day, the more you'll realize how much you both want and need it.

It's the same with listening. When you patiently listen to your partner as she talks about her day or her feelings, your distraction-hungry brain may want to jump to your smartphone or start daydreaming about sports or work. But the more you listen, the more sincerely interested you'll become in what your partner is going through. Before you know it, you'll be asking her questions to hear more!

Listening is a great way to give emotional support, but so is talking. Learn to express your feelings to your wife or partner, too. Are you nervous about the health of the baby? Are you scared you'll make a crummy dad? Tell her about how you feel!

That honest, two-way conversation is essential to fortifying your relationship as a couple—strengthening that second R in P-A-R-R.

#5: BE UNDERSTANDING

Okay, listening and giving emotional support when your wife is saying and doing things that make sense to you is easy. But the time will come when she acts in ways you don't understand. Chalk it up to stress or hormones or a combination of the two, but the day will come when you'll be puzzled by your wife. When that happens, it's easy for your patience to wear thin.

Remember I mentioned that I accused my wife of being a completely different person? You see, on that day, she was acting so out of touch and emotional that I simply couldn't understand her anymore! Then the cherry on top was when it was time for dinner.

I'd been trying to cook as many nights a week as my work would allow. And I'd picked up a great recipe for some beef fajitas. (By the way, if you're learning to cook, fajitas are a great starting dish because they are really easy to learn to make. And they're delicious!)

I'd told Linda about my plans to make fajitas. She was stoked because one of our favorite places to eat was a Mexican food restaurant.

But that night, after I'd slaved away over a hot stove, making my first-ever fajitas, when I set them down on the table, Linda pushed her plate away with her nose wrinkled in disgust.

"What did you put in those?" she asked me. "They smell like bleach!"

Needless to say, I was a little hurt and offended. "Bleach?" I said. "What are you talking about?"

I tasted the fajitas, and they were delicious! But Linda couldn't stomach them. The smell made her nauseous.

I didn't take it well. I was confused and hurt. After all, Linda had loved the idea of me making fajitas. She'd told me they smelled wonderful just a few minutes earlier. I certainly hadn't added some last-minute bleach as seasoning.

So, I accused her of being a different person. I wanted to know where *my* Linda was, the Linda who wanted to eat those delicious fajitas!

Let me tell you right now: that was NOT the right thing to say just then. I was in the doghouse, for sure.

The lesson: be understanding and be reasonable. Respect that your partner's taste, smell, or mood could change at the drop of a hat.

In my case, I wasn't looking to quit my job and become a chef and open my own fajitas-only restaurant. I'd lost sight of the fact that I was only learning to cook in the first place because I wanted to be supportive of my pregnant wife.

So, yeah, be reasonable. Don't fly off the handle. Learn to adjust to the changes along with your wife. Your wife or partner isn't being moody on purpose. It's the pregnancy. And fajitas taste just as good reheated the next day. No harm, no foul.

#6: FINALLY, FIND WAYS TO DOTE ON HER

Being supportive can also mean going that extra mile to make a romantic gesture or help her relieve some stress. Run her a hot bath every once in a while or learn to give great massages. Take her out to dinner or plan a little romantic getaway.

Tell her she's beautiful and mean it. She's going through all these changes, physical changes in her body, and she may not feel very beautiful on some days. Don't wait for her to ask. Just tell her! Tell her you love her!

Look, I'm a guy and writing to you, another guy. So, I'm not going to get all mushy on you. You know what to do to make her feel special. So be there for her and dote on her. Treat those nine months of the pregnancy as if they were the first nine months of a new romantic relationship. That means being romantic and a gentleman at every opportunity.

And while you're at it, make sure you take some time to relax yourself. Do things together you can both enjoy in order to relieve stress. That way, you'll both benefit.

A LITTLE EXTRA SUPPORT GOES A LONG WAY

Returning to the scene from the start of this chapter, I had an important choice to make. For about a month in the middle of the pregnancy, my wife had terrible nausea and had trouble sleeping. Although she didn't expect me to stay up half the night with her, I did my best to be there for her.

I'll never forget the look on her face in the bathroom that night when I offered to get her some water and stay up with her. She knew it was hard on me, just like it was hard on her. She knew I had work in the morning and was stressed about that big report that was due. But she also didn't want to face the trials of pregnancy alone.

On those nights, what she needed was not to be alone. She needed emotional support.

And if you give that support to your wife or partner, you'll be strengthening your relationship, and you'll be doing everything you can to make sure your partner is happier and healthier.

Of course, there is so much more than emotional support. In the following chapter, we'll also discuss what you can do to support your partner's physical health. That's right; it's time to talk about exercise!

3

ENCOURAGE HER TO EXERCISE

I was so mad that I wanted to punch someone. The problem was, I knew I had no one to blame but myself, and punching myself in the face would probably just land me in the crazy house. Nonetheless, I was still screaming mad as I stood shirtless in the bathroom, looking at myself in the mirror.

I had a spare tire. Love handles. It was embarrassing. And don't even get me started about the man boobs!

We were two months into our second pregnancy, and I was developing the dreaded *dad bod*. No, forget dad bod; I was literally turning into my own dad. With another thirty pounds, a bit of gray in my hair, and an embarrassingly colorful golf shirt, my dad and I would look like twins.

I'd managed to avoid gaining weight when we had our first, Cody. Money was tight, so having a gym membership was a thing of the past. But I set up a little home gym in the back of the garage and started working out almost every morning. I'd read somewhere that you should do thirty-four pull-ups a day, which averages out to about a thousand a month, so I made sure to do that. And it worked! I managed to stay in shape (mostly) as a dad.

But now? Things were different.

If money was tight with one kid, expecting a second made our budget even tighter. I was stressed and busy, and I let the workout schedule slip a little.

Now, there is this thing called Couvade syndrome, otherwise known as sympathetic pregnancy. This is when men actually experience some of the symptoms of pregnancy along with their expecting wives. Weight gain is one of those symptoms. Other guys might experience shifts in mood and hormones or even morning sickness. I don't know if I can blame a sympathetic pregnancy or just plain stress, but, as I looked at my bloated and pudgy body in the mirror that morning, I didn't much care why it was happening. I was much more determined to kiss the dad bod goodbye as quickly as possible.

Now, why am I talking about dad bods and weight gain and exercise? You may be as vain as I am and care about that stuff, too. And that's totally okay, but the big message I have for you is this: however important you think exercise is for you as a dad, it's ten times more important for your pregnant wife or partner.

In this chapter, we're going to talk about why and how you should help your wife get regular exercise. We'll also talk about what exercises are good for her and which are no-nos.

But first, a big-time disclaimer.

TALK TO YOUR DOCTOR ABOUT EXERCISE

This may seem like a no-brainer, but it's a really important step. And, surprisingly enough, just like with nutrition, doctors won't usually bring this stuff up unless you ask.

So, my recommendation is this: ask. Ask early and ask often. Bring up exercise and diet at every checkup. Report what you're doing, what you're thinking of doing, and any problems your wife or partner encounters while exercising.

Why is it super important to talk to her doctor about this stuff? Because there are certain conditions some women develop during pregnancy (like a weak cervix or low placenta) that would make many kinds of exercises very dangerous for her and/or the baby.

So, while it's true that the exercises I'll talk about later are great for pregnant women in most cases, don't even think about assuming they'll be good for your wife or partner until you've cleared your exercise goals with your gynecologist or obstetrician.

Okay, with that out of the way, what are the benefits of exercise for pregnant women?

HOW EXERCISE HELPS

In movies and TV, pregnant women are almost always seen as laying down or crashing on the couch, feet up, with a few extra pillows in just the right places to ease their aches and pains. In fact, for the most part, pregnant women are shown as largely inactive. And, yes, it's good for your wife or partner to get some extra rest during pregnancy, as we've already mentioned in this book. She may also need to sleep more than usual because growing a baby is a lot of work for the body.

But, at the same time, unless she has a condition that prevents her from being able to work out (again, see your doctor for more information on that), then daily exercise is actually full of excellent benefits for her.

For example, exercise may prevent your wife or partner from getting gestational diabetes (a unique form of diabetes that develops during pregnancy and is dangerous for both the mother and the baby), along with other health problems. On top of that, regular exercise will help her build strength and stamina, which can help her fight discomfort and fatigue during pregnancy. Exercise will also prepare her physically for labor and delivery.

Another huge benefit of exercise is stress relief. We've already discussed how dangerous stress and anxiety are to your physical health. Even a simple twenty-minute walk a day can reduce stress by a ton. That, in turn, benefits your heart and vascular health, lowers your blood sugar, and boosts your immune system—all great benefits for everyone all the time, but especially for pregnant women.

Exercise can also help both you and her with your self-image. While you might, like me, have nightmares of growing a beer belly and turning into your old man, your wife or partner may also feel very negative about her body, especially as her belly, ankles, and everything else swells. Some regular exercise can help her to feel better about herself. But also be sure to remind her that it's healthy and natural for her to put on extra body fat during pregnancy. Her body's just storing up energy to grow that baby and take care of it after birth!

So, as you can see, while rest is important during pregnancy, so is exercise. In fact, getting regular exercise throughout the pregnancy is a great way to boost your partner's health, which will lead to a healthier baby, too.

So, what can you do about it? As a follower of the Dad Code, you'll want to encourage and support her throughout the pregnancy by working out with her, of course!

THE DAD CODE AND EXERCISE

Remember P-A-R-R? The P stands for "partner." So you can't park yourself on the couch, put on one of Netflix's many cheesy action movies from the 80s, and tell your wife or partner to go out and exercise alone, right? According to the Dad Code, you absolutely must be her workout partner. Why not start with a twenty-minute walk in the evenings? Or a few leisurely laps at the local community swimming pool?

The A in P-A-R-R stands for "age," as in "adapt what you do to the age of the baby." The same applies to what stage of the pregnancy you're in. On a larger scale, think of the A as standing for "adaptability."

Some things may be comfortable for your partner early in the pregnancy, but as her belly grows, that extra weight will throw off her balance and cause fatigue and pain, so what you do to stay active will have to adapt to those changes. (And, need I repeat it? Talk to your doctor every step of the way to make sure what you're doing isn't putting the baby at risk.)

Finally, the double-R comes into play, too. When you work out together, like taking walks or doing stretches together, you'll have the opportunity to continue to build on your relationship as partners.

Curtis, I get it, you may be thinking. *Exercise is good for both of us. I'm on board. But what exercises are good for us to do?*

What a great question! Let's talk about that next.

GREAT PREGNANCY EXERCISE IDEAS

I'm not going to tell you again that you should run all this by your wife's doctor (but you totally should) because I think we've already established that. But here are some exercises that Linda and I have tried and really enjoy.

Walking. This is obviously the easiest exercise to start doing. A leisurely walk around the block in the morning or evening is a great way to start. Some experts also suggest jogging, especially if your partner was already a jogger before pregnancy. This is also the best relationship-building exercise, in my opinion. When you go for a brisk walk or slow jog, you get to talk together and laugh at inside jokes. Of course, with jogging or running, as with just about any exercise, it's best not to overdo it.

Indoor aerobics or dance classes. This kind of thing may not be your cup of tea, and your wife may be fine doing this with her girlfriends rather than with you. But there are tons of aerobics classes that are either pregnancy-safe or even specifically designed for pregnant women.

Aerobic machines. These may include stationary bikes, treadmills, rowing machines, ellipticals, and the like. Unless you have a much better-paying job than I do, don't worry about filling up a credit card to buy something like this, though. In my experience, most people that buy this kind of equipment don't end up using it very much. It would be way cheaper to pay for a gym or health club membership for a few months. Many places offer special sign-up deals or couple discounts. A great thing about those memberships—as long as they don't try to lock you in on some kind of contract—is you can cancel them if you stop going.

Pilates, yoga, and tai chi. Okay, I may be showing my ignorance in listing all of these things as a single group. The only one Linda and I have tried is yoga. Our community hospital sponsored a pregnancy yoga class during our second pregnancy, and we went because it was relatively inexpensive. But these kinds of workouts help you build strength, stamina, and flexibility, all while being very chill and low impact.

EXERCISES TO AVOID WHEN PREGNANT

Some exercises are definitely a bad idea, especially as your wife or partner progresses in the pregnancy. Here are a few we stumbled upon, either in my reading or because our doctor told us to avoid them.

Jumping. Okay, jumping isn't really an exercise in itself, but a lot of exercises and sports involve bouncing or jumping up and down. These are generally a no-no because they are hard on the growing baby inside the belly.

Sit-ups and crunches. Obviously, this would also be traumatic for the baby. Pregnancy is not the time to try and get (or maintain) those rock-hard abs.

Risky activities. Any activity that could be jarring on the body or where there is a risk of falling should probably be avoided, especially after the first few months. Think skiing, mountain biking, or horseback riding.

Overly strenuous exercises. Pregnancy is also not the time to try and beat your personal best in deadlifting, obviously. Any activity that feels overly strenuous on the body is probably a bad idea. Your wife or partner will have to listen to her body. The key is to be active without pushing yourself too hard.

Activities in extreme weather. Depending on where you live, and the time of year, some activities may be a bad idea. Obviously, going jogging on a cool sixty-degree day is very different from going for a run during a snowstorm. And the same goes for extreme heat and humidity. When Linda was pregnant with our second child, Liberty, her doctor warned her against doing too much in the extreme heat of summer. (Liberty was born on July 4th, which is how she got her name in the first place.) It turns out that high heat and humidity strain the body in ways you can't see. Your heart works much harder in extreme temperatures, for example.

As you can tell, a lot of this stuff is common sense. And it also really depends on what your wife or partner was used to doing before getting pregnant. If she hit the gym for an hour a day and ran marathons on the weekends, she'll be able to do a lot more during the pregnancy than a gal that was relatively inactive before getting pregnant. The key is not to do too much too soon.

That said, even a competitive athlete will have to adapt her exercise routine when pregnant. Many exercises like yoga, weight training, aerobics, or running can continue into pregnancy, but they may have to be adjusted in certain ways to make the activities "baby safe."

COUPLES THAT WORK OUT TOGETHER STAY TOGETHER

I have to admit that I was a selfish exerciser during our first pregnancy. I did a lot of exercising on my own, fighting off the dad bod, and the most I did for Linda was suggest she book a weekly Zumba class down the street. But give me a break! I was still developing the Dad Code and certainly hadn't mastered it yet.

Even during the second pregnancy, when I had the scare of my life looking in the mirror that morning, my first impulse to exercise was actually quite vain and selfish. But then I made a decision that turned out to be the best thing I could do: I decided to include Linda in my workout ideas.

We started exploring exercise activities together. Of course, we had a frank talk with her OB/GYN, and we started walking almost every day. We also signed up for those yoga classes I mentioned earlier. The room was mostly pregnant women of various sizes, along with a few supportive dads like myself.

As we worked out together, we had to really adjust our schedules to make it work. But it was so worth it. We had a great time together. We laughed a lot (especially trying to get those yoga poses; I'm glad no one brought a camera to those classes), and we both started to feel better about our bodies.

And you know the best part? Both Linda and the baby were healthy throughout the pregnancy. As a dad, that's the best miracle you can wish for. Liberty came two full weeks early, ruining our Fourth of July plans and scaring us both half to death, but the labor was easier with her than it had been with our first kid. And when I say it was probably a good diet and exercise that helped, I'm not just guessing. Linda's doctor said the same thing!

And I know you're dying to know, so I'll tell you. I ditched the dad bod, and you can too! I still do a thousand pull-ups a month, by the way, and I can't suggest that enough.

So, get active with your wife or partner. Work together to take her health seriously because that means you're also taking the baby's health seriously. And, I don't want to get too big picture here, but people these days are unhealthier than ever before. What a great culture to establish within your family from the very start—a family tradition of taking health seriously by eating smart and making time for exercise, family time, and outdoor activities.

Some might say that's one of the best gifts you can give your kid, and you won't get any arguments from me!

Now, while eating right and exercising are super important, they aren't the only aspects of your wife's health you want to be proactive on. In the following chapter, we'll talk about your partner's other medical needs. We'll also see how you can work with your partner and healthcare professionals to optimize both her and the baby's health.

REVIEW REQUEST

Enjoyed the Book?

Leave a 1-Click Review!

Reviews are like gold for authors.
Would you please take a few seconds and leave me a
review on Amazon?
I would be super happy.

Scan the QR code below to leave a quick review

4

PAY ATTENTION TO HER
MEDICAL NEEDS

I've always been something of an overachiever. That doesn't mean I'm more successful or talented than others. True story—a friend of mine in college is now a retired billionaire because he founded a startup while I just got hired at one. He sold his company and lives off-grid in Colorado like all the coolest eccentric billionaires do these days. I'm in middle management and barely scrape by every month. So I'm certainly not the most successful guy around.

But I do have a tendency to take on more than I can handle. I'm a perfectionist, too, so I'm always driven to get things right.

Maybe you have a similar streak in you. Maybe you don't. But, either way, let me make something really clear right now: no matter how much you read and study, no matter how great a dad you plan to be, you cannot do the job of a doctor. You can't (and shouldn't try to) replace a good healthcare provider.

Even if you happen to be an OB/GYN—a doctor specializing in pregnancy and delivering babies—you probably shouldn't be caring for your own wife unless you're in a small town and you're the only option for a hundred miles.

If you want to take care of your wife or partner's health, you absolutely need to seek professional medical help, and you need to take full advantage of that help. This chapter will help you learn how you can do that.

So if you were sick and tired of me telling you to ask your doctor about things in the last chapter on exercise, well, I've got some bad news for you. This chapter is all about talking to your doctor. (And I'm calling them *your* doctor for a reason, which I'll get to in a moment.)

First, let's talk about what kind of doctor you need to find and when. Then we'll get into some specific ways that you—the dad—can actively support your wife or partner's medical and health needs.

HOW TO CHOOSE THE RIGHT HEALTH CARE PROVIDER

By the time you picked up this book, you might have already gone to see a doctor about the pregnancy. But if you're reading these words with that surprising positive pregnancy test still fresh in your memory, then let's talk about the big choice you and your partner will have to make now: who will provide for her medical needs throughout the pregnancy?

Here are a few key options:

Your family doctor. Especially if you live in a very small town, your best or only option might be your family practitioner. Many family doctors are very experienced in delivering babies, even if that is not actually their specialty. The advantage of sticking with your family doctor is that both you and your wife will probably already be very familiar with them and have a good relationship with them. Plus, that same doctor will probably also be giving the child regular checkups as they grow up.

Her gynecologist (who is also an OB/GYN). Once again, this is a great choice because your wife may already be familiar with her gynecologist and have a relationship with them. Many gynecologists are licensed obstetricians as well, so they can certainly take care of her throughout the pregnancy and deliver the child.

An obstetrician. An obstetrician is a doctor who specializes entirely in pregnancy and delivery. Obviously, there are advantages to having a specialist because they are most likely up on all the latest medicines and procedures concerning child-birthing. On the other hand, humans have been having kids for like a bazillion years, so most of it isn't exactly cutting-edge stuff. (Just don't tell your doctor I said that!)

Certified nurse-midwife. Another option is to choose an experienced and certified midwife. This person specializes in everything related to pregnancy and delivery. If you go with a midwife, she'll still need to have a doctor on call in case a C-section is necessary. (That's when they remove the baby through surgery.)

Any of these options can totally work for you. It all depends on what options are available to you and whom you feel most comfortable with. Fun fact: Linda and I were going to go with a midwife during her first pregnancy. We had chats with her, but—in a surprise plot twist—she called us back with the wonderful news that she was also pregnant. So, we all decided that her delivering a baby while so close to having a baby herself might make for a fun setup for a sitcom or something . .

. but it probably wasn't a good idea. We ended up going with an OB/GYN highly recommended by the midwife.

When choosing a health care provider, don't downplay the personality side of things. A doctor might have a wall plastered with a hundred certifications and have more little pins on his white coat than a five-star general, but if he's difficult to talk to or doesn't make you feel comfortable, don't hesitate to look for other options.

You want someone you can have open and frank conversations with, someone you feel you can trust. And, even more importantly, you want someone that will take the time to talk with you and put you at ease. Doctors that treat you like cattle, stamping your butt and prodding you down the line by calling "Next!" may be highly qualified to deliver babies, but will they give you the emotional support and practical advice you crave? If not, look for someone who will.

CHECKUPS, CHECKUPS, CHECKUPS!

Did you like going to the doctor as a kid? If you were like me, you might have been scared stiff of the dreaded checkup, especially when it was time to go to the dentist. Well, as an expecting couple, you'll have to get used to doctor's offices, because you'll be in them quite a bit.

As soon as your wife or partner thinks she's pregnant, you may decide to see a doctor to confirm. Then, once confirmed that a baby is on the way, you'll want to choose a health care provider and make an appointment. Don't wait too long for this! I'd say try and schedule an appointment as soon as you can, although some doctors won't want to have that first prenatal checkup until about eight weeks into the pregnancy. (As an FYI, "prenatal" means "during the pregnancy.")

A healthy expecting mother will probably be expected to have a checkup every four weeks at first. Then, at around week twenty-eight, that may change to every two weeks. Then, at around week thirty-six, the doctor may want to see her every week until delivery. Of course, if there are any complications along the way, that will probably mean even more visits to the doctor (or even to more than one doctor, depending on the situation).

Complications! you might be thinking with a big, nervous lump in your throat. I know how you feel because I've been there—just thinking about something going wrong used to make my head spin. But it doesn't have to be that scary, which is why you'll want to talk to your doctor often and frankly and go through whatever tests he suggests.

Think about it this way:

When I was young, we used to burn CDs of our favorite music or even make copies of a great album a school friend had bought at Walmart or the mall. If you remember the process of burning CDs, sometimes something would go wrong. Suddenly, your PC would spit the CD out, displaying an error message on the monitor. Not only did you not get the copied album you wanted, but now that CD was ruined, trash! You'd have to put a new blank CD into the drive and start over.

Pregnancy is **not** like burning a CD, in which any little glitch in the system ruins the whole process. Your subconscious mind worries that it is, but it totally isn't.

Instead, think of your wife's pregnancy as a long voyage on a ship in the ocean.

You have a destination in mind, a faraway port the ship wants to get to. Let's call the port town Healthy Baby Bay. You have maps and a compass, and you're heading straight for Healthy Baby Bay. But it's a long voyage—nine whole months long—and the waters can get rough sometimes.

Maybe a strong wind or unexpected shift in currents starts to push you a bit off course. Or maybe there's a big storm ahead, and you decide to adjust course to go around it. None of those things mean the ship won't get to Healthy Baby Bay. They just mean you'll have to make some adjustments along the way.

So, in the same way, pregnancy has lots of potential issues that can come up. Doctors sometimes give these issues really scary names like *preeclampsia* or *gestational diabetes*. But, just like getting knocked off course in the ship, the earlier you recognize a condition (or being at risk for a certain condition), the more manageable the situation is.

That's why all the regular checkups are so important. Along the way, your doctor may ask you questions or perform certain prenatal tests. They may adjust your partner's diet or say some exercises are off-limits until the end of the pregnancy. This is all part of the process. It's about adjusting the course.

With your doctor's help, you can keep your sights squarely set on Healthy Baby Bay!

THE DAD CODE AND MEDICAL NEEDS

Earlier in this chapter, I mentioned "your doctor." It's not "her doctor." That doctor, OB/GYN, or midwife belongs to *both of you*. As a dad wishing to follow the Dad Code, keeping in mind the P at the start that stands for "partner," you need to see that doctor and those doctor visits as a team effort and a responsibility for both of you as a couple.

Does this mean you'll be able to make it to 100% of all checkups with your wife? Maybe not. If you're the primary breadwinner in the family, you have to keep the employer happy, too. But don't let work or anything else become the excuse not to be involved in your partner's medical journey.

I've worked full-time at a medium-sized tech company through both pregnancies, and I wasn't always able to get the time off for every minor checkup, mommy class, and a sit-down with the prenatal nutritionist. But I was able to make arrangements to be at most appointments, even if that meant adjusting the time of my lunch break and skipping a meal so we could talk to the doc together.

If you explain to your boss or business partner that work-life balance is important to you and that you're trying to follow the Dad Code and be a good partner to your pregnant wife, you might be surprised how much flexibility you'll be granted to have your cake and eat it, too.

And being a partner doesn't just mean being there. It means paying close attention to everything the doctor says. It means piping up with questions and asking for clarification. Two heads are better than one, right? So, if you and your wife both ask questions and make sure you understand what's happening, you'll walk away from each visit empowered to make the best possible decisions for her and the baby's health—together.

About questions: don't be embarrassed to bring up sensitive stuff. And make sure your partner isn't embarrassed either. Have questions about sex during pregnancy? Ask away. What about other private stuff like constipation, hemorrhoids and just about anything that has the word "vaginal" in front of it? Don't hesitate to ask.

Unless your doctor was a medical student up until about five minutes ago, and the ink on their certification is still drying, it'll be almost impossible to bring up or ask something they haven't heard before. So don't be afraid to ask even the most embarrassing and dumb-sounding questions.

On top of that, as first-time parents, you or your wife may get nervous about the littlest things. Throughout our first pregnancy, Linda was terrified of every little change in her body—the baby's kicking too much or not kicking enough, one breast feels different than the other, or (I kid you not) she keeps dreaming of snakes. Don't let those little anxieties fester in your heads. Just bring it up with the doctor, let them smile that knowing little smile, and reassure you that everything's fine.

Or, on the other hand, you never know when some minor observation you or your wife makes raises your doctor's eyebrows and prompts some new prenatal test or a change in diet or vitamins. Then you'll really be glad you brought it up!

The lesson here: work together as a team—you, your wife, and your health care provider. And don't be afraid to ask questions, get clarification, or share any fears or doubts you might have. In the doctor's office, knowledge is power!

LET'S TALK ABOUT DIET

Another way you can work with your partner during pregnancy is by supporting her diet. Now, when I say diet, I don't mean going to Weight Watchers or taking up some fad diet to lose weight. I mean making healthy eating choices.

Doctors will often encourage her to eat more calories than normal. They may suggest certain vitamins or foods, and, as we'll see below, they may recommend avoiding other things that could cause problems in the pregnancy.

Why not try to make some healthier decisions yourself during the pregnancy? I mean, you don't have to take prenatal vitamins, but planning healthier meals will benefit both of you, and it will be easier for your wife to be healthy if she has your support along the way.

Eating healthy doesn't mean trying to avoid gaining weight. Women *should* gain some pounds, especially during the second half of the pregnancy. In fact, an otherwise slim woman will put on more weight than one that was already a little hefty.

Making healthy decisions includes (as we mentioned before) cutting out alcohol, tobacco, and other drugs. This is a no-brainer, right? And, as I mentioned in a previous chapter, the best thing you can do to support her is to cut those things out, too.

But here are some other things pregnant women generally need to avoid. Ask your doctor about the following foods/substances for more details:

Most (if not all) over-the-counter medicines. Many over-the-counter medicines are a no-no for pregnant women. Even if the instructions on the back of a medicine label don't say you shouldn't take it if pregnant, it's best to talk to your doctor about any and all prescriptions your wife is on to make double sure.

Raw or unpasteurized dairy. This may include unpasteurized milk or very soft cheeses. Unpasteurized juices and apple cider are also a bad idea.

Raw eggs. And that would include something that includes raw eggs, like a nice chocolate mousse.

Raw or undercooked meats, including "cured" deli meats. This would include raw fish and shellfish, which are generally considered no-nos. Processed meats like hot dogs or pastrami are generally considered risky and should be avoided, too.

If you do a bunch of research about fish and shellfish, you'll get conflicting information on them. On the one hand, lots of seafood is a great source of omega-3 fatty acids. The omega-3s are super healthy, especially for a developing baby. But, at the same time, there is a lot of mercury in seafood that can be very harmful to a developing baby's brain. However, some kinds of fish, especially farmed fish, are naturally low in mercury, such as salmon.

Of course, if you have any questions, you should discuss your concerns with your doctor.

A WORD ABOUT VACCINES

Vaccines are a hot political topic these days. I don't intend to beat one drum or another here. But your doctor may suggest certain vaccines for your pregnant wife.

Of course, taking any vaccine is a personal decision. But do your own research about it and raise any objections you have in a calm conversation with your doctor. They can help you make a decision that will benefit your partner and unborn child.

All in all, keep in mind that you don't have to do everything. Being a super dad doesn't mean you have to study to be a doctor on the side. But it does mean being involved in your wife's medical journey. As you do, you'll be able to work together to keep the bow of the ship pointed directly for Healthy Baby Bay.

As that journey reaches its end, however, tensions will mount, and excitement levels will be at an all-time high. As the due date nears, it will be time to prepare for delivery. That's what we'll cover in the following chapter.

5

MAKE A SUCCESS OF THE DELIVERY

It was a sweltering summer, and Linda was—in her own words and not mine—as big as a blimp. Our second child, a girl, was due in a couple of weeks, and as July Fourth came up, we decided to plan a big family fun day out at the lake. I'm talking hot dogs, ice cream, and fireworks—the whole shebang!

We drove out to the lake, more than an hour from our house. We'd booked a nice hotel in a nearby town, not exactly the penthouse at the Four Seasons but a luxury suite by our standards. They even had a big tub with jacuzzi jets, and Linda was looking forward to a weekend soaking in that tub and using the jets to relieve her constant back pain.

But first, the big cookout and fireworks!

ept Linda started complaining of some discomfort not long after arriving at the cookout spot. We didn't think anything of it at the time. Most people don't realize that pregnant women have contractions on and off throughout the pregnancy and not just in the hours just before labor. Linda's back and belly were tightening up a bit, so she went for a little walk up the lake shore and back.

Meanwhile, I was getting the charcoal heated up. I'd packed away some fancy steaks and some alcohol-free champagne that Linda didn't know about. I wanted her to really have a wonderful time this weekend because we knew that, come Monday, she'd be 100% in *preparation for labor* mode.

It was a beautiful day. Even though we were in the middle of a heat wave, the breeze off the lake was cool and refreshing. I was very excited to have a great lunch, help our son Cody fire off some fireworks, and then pack up early to get to the hotel to start the relaxing phase of our weekend getaway.

Except we didn't get to do any of that! Linda returned from her walk with some exciting—if not confusing—news: her water had broken!

We immediately called Linda's doctor, who was just as surprised as we were. Linda started having contractions. I knew how to time them (which we'll talk about later in this chapter), so I could text message the doctor with updates.

Another thing most people don't know because it's portrayed much more dramatically in movies is that a pregnant woman's water can break up to a couple of days before going into labor. Hollywood makes it sound like the baby is just hours away when the water breaks, but the truth is much slower and less certain.

And our baby was almost two full weeks away from her due date. Surely there wasn't any urgency, right?

Except I sent the doctor the updated contraction times, and he responded with the message I knew deep in my gut we'd receive: "Get back to town now. I'll meet you at the hospital."

Our second child was a bit of a surprise in that way. She was ready to come early, and she wasn't going to take "no" for an answer. Luckily, I'd packed our delivery bag. So, we packed up our stuff and headed back to town.

The fancy steak and the hot tub would have to wait!

Labor can come at the least expected of moments, a lesson we learned the hard way with our second child. That's why you absolutely want to be ready for delivery.

And I do mean *you* need to be ready. The Dad Code absolutely compels us as fathers to be there to support our partners through this magical, scary, and challenging time. So how can you prepare for "The Big Day?" What are the signs that labor is beginning? How can you support your wife or partner during labor and delivery? And what can you do to help her in the moments, days, and weeks after the baby is born?

That's what this chapter is all about, so let's get started.

HOW TO PREPARE FOR LABOR AND DELIVERY

Labor is a stressful time. Your partner will experience periods of discomfort or pain. It can take much longer than expected, sometimes even several hours, and you'll both be holding your breath through it, praying that nothing goes wrong.

That said, there is a lot you can do to prepare for childbirth. Let's look at some key things you can do to help ensure the delivery process is as comfortable and stress-free as possible.

Get educated. We've talked about the importance of equipping yourself with knowledge when it comes to pregnancy, but the same is equally true when it comes to labor and delivery. Read up on what actually happens to the woman's body during labor. Read first-hand experiences from mothers, fathers, and even doctors. The things you learn will help you with the following step, too.

Prepare your labor kit (or go-bag). Pack a bag for labor and keep it within reach at all times. Even when Linda and I were sure our second baby's delivery was two weeks away, we didn't dare pack for a weekend out of the house without having our delivery go-bag in the car. You'll want changes of comfortable clothes for both you and her, as well as massage tools, scented oils, and whatever else you've decided together will help her relax between contractions. Of course, just in case you drop your phone down a well right as labor begins, keep emergency numbers—like those of relatives, friends, your doctor, and your hospital—printed out and in a pocket in your go-bag.

Join a class. We've talked about pregnancy classes before, but it bears repeating. There are also special birthing classes designed for women approaching their due date. These will teach her things like breathing exercises and even self-hypnosis. Attend with her because the class will teach you how to massage her or help her stay comfortable through labor.

Stay positive and relaxed. This is a more mental thing, and it's something you can start doing from the start of the pregnancy. Studies show that women who are less stressed and more positive about their delivery have shorter and less painful labors. So, avoid the negative comments. Social media is full of horror stories of things going wrong during childbirth. Avoid those like the plague. As the due date nears, keep her relaxed. Practice relaxing breathing exercises and mindfulness meditation together. Yoga is also great for this.

Consider hiring professional delivery support. There are these delivery coaches, called *doulas*, who provide non-medical emotional and physical support during labor and delivery. Studies show that these highly trained professionals, while not being a doctor or even a midwife, actually help women to have a shorter and less painful labor. So, you might want to look into one ahead of time to see if it's for you.

Of course, everything we've talked about so far in this book prepares both you and your wife for delivery. When you've exercised throughout the pregnancy and been there to support her both emotionally and physically, you've done a lot to support her ability to actually enjoy the experience of giving birth. But your job as a partner (remember the P in P-A-R-R, right?) doesn't end when you get her to the hospital.

What can you do to support your partner through the child birthing process? We'll definitely get to that. But first, let's talk about some of the signs that labor is imminent.

HOW TO KNOW WHEN THE BABY IS COMING

If our second pregnancy taught me anything, it's that you can't depend on the due date.

Cody, our first, came two days late. It was like he was too comfortable in there and didn't want to come out. His labor lasted several hours, too, the classic reluctant baby.

But our second child was the exact opposite of her big brother. She was too excited to get started on life. So, she came two weeks early and was born two hours into labor.

Babies can be pretty unpredictable. Who knew? While you can't set your clock to delivery, some signs can let you know the baby is on its way. Let's talk about a few of them.

A nesting wife. As we've discussed, women need more and more rest as they get closer to the due date. Their belly is larger and heavier, so it makes sense that they are tired most of the time. But many pregnant women go into what the professionals call "nesting mode" when the baby is a few days away from coming. She'll suddenly have a new burst of energy. She'll have this sudden maternal instinct to clean the house, prepare the baby's room, and cook meals. Looking back, a couple of days before that July Fourth, Linda was doing this. She spent days reorganizing the baby's room and crib. And I had to keep reminding her to take it easy and stop cleaning everything in sight. Of course, I didn't know how to recognize "nesting" at the time.

A lowering baby belly. Medical professionals will sometimes call this "the baby dropping," which sounds scarier than it is. In the hours or days before labor, the baby starts to shift position. Your wife will feel "lighter" and be able to breathe easier. But the belly may sag lower than usual, and she may start to walk with an exaggerated waddle. A lowering baby may also put extra pressure on the bladder, so she may start going to the bathroom more than usual, too.

The water breaks. As we said before, movies make this into a big, dramatic thing that happens right as labor is about to begin. How many scenes have you seen where the pregnant mother is in the middle of something and, *SPLASH,* the water breaks, and she almost immediately goes into labor? But the reality of it all isn't so dramatic as Hollywood makes it out to be—at least not all the time. Sometimes it's just a trickle of water and not a comical splash. Sometimes it happens several hours or even days before labor begins. (After the water breaks, the baby is more susceptible to infections, so doctors will often want to induce labor within a few days of the water breaking, just to be on the safe side.) Sometimes the water never breaks at all! In that case, the baby will come out still encased in a "sack" of fluid, and the doctor or midwife will have to tear the sack open to get the baby out. (Don't worry, it may sound gross, but it's not a big deal.)

Contractions and lower back pain. We all know contractions are a sign of labor, right? Well, not always. Contractions can actually happen throughout the pregnancy. The body has to get ready for delivery, which involves a lot of pushing. Those muscles need to be prepared to push the baby out, so contractions are actually a way of waking the muscles up and strengthening them. Early cramping and contractions will often go away if your partner changes positions, walks around, or lays down. When contractions become regularly spaced and refuse to go away, then you know labor is getting near.

Let me reiterate that point because it's really important. Your pregnant partner may have contractions from time to time throughout the pregnancy. As the due date nears, she may start feeling stronger contractions—the muscles in her belly and back suddenly squeezing tight and cramping. That may be alarming and cause you to rush to the hospital, only to discover that it's a false alarm. To distinguish between false and legit labor, have your partner walk around or change positions. If the contractions stop, then everything is fine, and the baby isn't coming. If the contractions are regular, however, and they refuse to go away, then it's much less likely to be a false alarm; call your doctor.

Stomach problems. Many women report nausea or diarrhea just before labor. This didn't happen in Linda's case, but it is fairly common.

Of course, whenever you experience any of these situations or a combination of them, it doesn't hurt to call your health care provider to report the symptoms. They can walk you through the process with the calm that comes from having delivered hundreds of babies in their careers.

So, let's say that labor begins. You've seen the signs and are sure the baby is coming. How can you support your wife during this chaotic but magical time? We'll get to that, but first, a note on timing contractions.

HOW TO TIME CONTRACTIONS

You've heard it in every movie with a delivery scene. The parents rush into the hospital, mid-labor. The doctor comes in with a big smile on their face. And they always ask the same question: "How far apart are the contractions?"

As a helpful and supporting dad, learning to time contractions is a must. So how do you do it? It's not the way you'd probably think.

First, think of a contraction as a wave. When your wife tells you she's starting to have a contraction, that means multiple muscles in her belly, groin, and lower back all start to tighten or cramp. It's a little painful, but it's mostly surprising because we're not used to our muscles bearing down like that without us controlling them. Think of that as the start of the wave, the point where the water rises and swells.

After a few minutes, the muscles will start to loosen. This can happen all at once or over the course of a few minutes. Your partner will breathe a sigh of relief. *Glad that's over!* That's the wave ending.

Then the wave will jump back up again as a new contraction starts. This can be half an hour later or just a couple of minutes later. Generally, when contractions get closer and closer together at a regular pace, that's a sure sign that the baby is ready to come out.

When it comes to timing contractions, you'd think you're supposed to count the amount of calm time in between waves. It sounds logical, right? After all, the doctors in the movies ask, "How far apart are her contractions?" But that's not the right way to do it.

Instead, to time contractions, count the amount of time from the start of one contraction to the start of the next contraction. In other words, you're counting how much time passes when the wave rises to when the next wave rises. This is the medical standard for timing them.

When you think about it, this really is the most accurate. After all, while contractions usually come on all at once—so it's easy to mark on the clock when they start —they may sometimes take a long time to calm down. If the muscles loosen gradually over several minutes, how are you supposed to mark on the clock when a contraction is officially over? Your wife or partner, as super in touch with her body as she may be, will always be much more accurate in telling when a contraction is starting than when it is ending.

So, for this reason, medical professionals have adopted the standard of timing contractions from the start of one to the start of the next one.

In your delivery go-bag, it may be good to keep a stopwatch, notebook, and pen. That way, you (or someone helping you) can keep track of the timing of contractions. You can always do it on your phone, of course. But I like to have a backup in case your phone decides to randomly explode at the same moment your wife goes into labor.

With that in mind, you'll be able to report on the timing of your partner's contractions with pretty good accuracy, meaning you'll be able to give a good report to your medical care provider when they ask that famous question: "How far apart are her contractions?"

HOW TO SUPPORT HER DURING DELIVERY

We rushed to the hospital with the efficiency of a Jason Bourne car chase scene. I'd rehearsed this route a thousand times and knew which side streets were the fastest and safest. Of course, I hadn't practiced speeding along the highway to get back to town first, but we got to the hospital in record time.

Linda was breathing deeply. Cody was in the back seat, helping me time the contractions.

The car skidded to a stop in front of the hospital. Cody was an awesome little helper, supporting his mom as she climbed out of the car while I ran for a nurse and wheelchair and returned for the go-bag. My parents were there, waiting for us, too, because we'd called them from the highway.

It was all coming together! We'd made it, and Linda was rushed immediately into a delivery room.

But my job wasn't done. In many ways, it was just beginning.

The old scene from movies of the father waiting outside in the waiting room for a doctor or nurse to come and inform him of the sex of their child is an outdated cliche. So is the scene of the father standing in the back of the delivery room, taking the world's most embarrassing video on a camcorder. These days, fathers are expected to be active participants in the delivery process.

Active participant? You might be screaming at me right now. You expect me to help deliver the baby?

By that, I don't mean that you'll be getting in the doctor's way. But there are several important ways to be a fantastic and active partner in the birthing process. We'll talk about some of those ways in a moment. But first, a caveat.

Caveat: You offer support ONLY when and where support is appreciated. In other words, you and your partner will have had several detailed conversations about what kind of support she wants from you during labor or delivery. You'll have a plan all sketched out. But then, when you're in the moment, her pain and hormones and emotional state will be taking the lead, and that's a lead you'll have to follow.

Some things you planned to do may not be appreciated anymore. Respect her wishes. She may ask you to do something you hadn't talked about previously. If you are able to do as she asks, then respect her wishes. Your job at this point is to support her because you love her and want what's best for her and your baby. It's not your job to boss her around. The medical professionals will be doing plenty of that because they know best. You're the support team—nothing more, nothing less.

So, you may or may not end up doing any or all of the things on the following list. You may end up doing something I don't mention here. And all of that is okay —as long as what you are doing is *supporting her.*

Okay, with that preamble out of the way, let's look at some of the things you may do to support your partner during labor and delivery.

Continue to time the contractions. Have a stopwatch or a stopwatch app handy and continue to time the contractions throughout the process. This can be helpful to both your wife and the doctors and nurses. Remember to time them from the start of one contraction to the start of another.

Stay calm. By this, I don't mean constantly reminding your wife to be calm. I tried that with our first delivery, and Linda didn't appreciate it very much. Instead, I mean become a beacon of calmness. Breathe easy, and don't raise your voice. Your stress will only add to hers, after all.

Be alert and helpful. Your partner will need to shift positions often. She'll ask for pillows. She'll need to get up and walk around between contractions. (Walking around is a very good idea. The more time you are out of bed, the better, unless your doctor has a medical reason to keep her in bed.) Whatever she needs or wherever she has to go, be there to help her.

Give a massage or make physical contact. Again, this is only a good idea if she is okay with it. If it bugs her, stop right away. But many women during labor appreciate someone massaging their back or legs or just holding their hand.

Keep her hydrated. Unless your wife is on an IV, then be sure to keep her hydrated by asking if she wants water on a regular basis. Also, offer to help her visit the bathroom between contractions.

Know when to step back. You want to be helpful and supportive. But either your wife or the doctors may request you step away from the bed at certain times.

Don't take this personally. Think of yourself as the world's greatest waiter. Your aim should be to appear the instant you are needed yet fade into the background when your presence isn't appreciated any longer.

Communicate with family and friends regularly. This is not an excuse to be on your phone with social media throughout the labor. But if there are close family members your partner really wants to be in the loop with, be sure to communicate with them often, if that means poking your head out the door to talk to them or messaging them every half hour. You'll also have the opportunity to relay words of love and encouragement back to your wife, which she will greatly appreciate.

Strap in for the long haul. Labor can be long, much longer than we sometimes expect. Cody really took his time to come into the world, and we were in that delivery room for hours and hours. I recently read that modern women are tending toward longer labor times than past generations! You have to remain patient, positive and supportive the whole time. Think of it as the role of a lifetime, and you're shooting for an Academy Award. You have an audience of one, and her good spirits are incredibly important to you!

As I said above, this is not an exhaustive list. You and your wife may talk and come up with additional ways you can support her throughout delivery.

Before we move on to taking care of the baby, we have one very important subject to cover first, and this subject involves you and your wife after delivery.

THE REST OF YOUR LIFE BEGINS NOW

The baby was ready to come and see the world, and we could both feel it. Linda's contractions were one after the other. I was there with her, holding her hand and walking her through breathing exercises. We got up and walked around as much as we could.

Then, before we knew it, the doctor told Linda the baby was ready. She pushed and pushed and pushed.

It felt like the world was spinning. And, on the inside, I was going completely crazy.

This is too fast, right?

What if something's wrong?

Will the baby be healthy? She's so early!

But I didn't let those fears out. I buried them in the deepest, darkest room of my mind dungeon and focused on keeping calm. The last thing anyone needed was me freaking out and adding to Linda's anxiety.

We were afraid, and we didn't feel ready. But it was all happening too fast for anyone to express those worries.

And then it was done! Our crying baby girl was passed from nurse to nurse, weighed, measured, cleaned up, blanketed, and passed back to Linda in a whirlwind of excitement, smiles and reassurances.

And the word your heart aches to hear above all others. I could have a lightsaber plunged into my chest at that moment, and I wouldn't care—as long as I heard that one, all-important seven-letter word: *healthy*.

"She looks healthy," the doctor said.

Healthy. I almost fainted.

Then Linda was smiling and crying at the same time. I held her close as we both looked down at our baby girl.

On July Fourth. We couldn't help but name her Liberty.

Childbirth is a miracle. It's cliche, I know. And everyone will say that to you because they heard it on TV. But once you go through it, once you experience it, you realize just how true those words are. The entire experience is magical.

Thankfully, Linda didn't experience anything more than some common baby blues with both of our children. I went ridiculously overboard with the support anyway. I took no chances.

Parenthood is a blessing, but delivery isn't the finish line. On the contrary, it's Chapter One. It's the first day of your new life as a *dad*.

You'll take your partner and baby home, and your life will be changed forever. Of course, at some point, reality will hit you. This little living thing is yours. That means it will be depending on you for everything. You'll look down at that bundle of joy, and the question will rise up from the pit of your stomach . . . *Now what?*

Chapter 7 is all about taking care of your newborn baby. In fact, most of the rest of the book will focus on your relationship with your newborn and how to be the best dad you can be for them. Before we get to that, however, there is one more important topic we need to tackle: both your wife's and your mental and emotional health.

How could having a baby lead directly to depression, despondence, and feelings of overwhelm? What can you do to take care of your partner and yourself in the days or weeks that follow delivery? We'll find out in the following chapter.

6

SUPPORTING HER (AND YOU) EMOTIONALLY AFTER CHILDBIRTH

The day your child is born is one of the happiest days of your life. Many fathers will tell you this because it's absolutely true. Maybe the pregnancy was planned and expected, or maybe the baby was a complete surprise that turned your lives upside down. Either way, the journey of pregnancy is thrilling and magical, and it all culminates with holding your child in your arms on that first day.

It's impossible to explain the love you'll feel for that child the second you lay eyes on them. It's like trying to explain to a computer what a chili dog tastes like.

But I do have a word of warning for you: while so, so many of the emotions you'll feel in that moment will be positive, don't be surprised when some powerful dark emotions start dancing in the pit of your stomach, too.

First of all, there's a great deal of fear. This tiny creature in your arms will now depend completely on you and your wife. It's fragile, vulnerable, and needy. Many, many parents I've talked to describe weeks or even months of sleepless nights, just worrying about what could happen *if* . . . On the other side of the if is an army of potential dangers. When Cody was less than a week old, I recorded in my journal how he felt to me like the flame of a candle. And even the slightest breeze could threaten that tiny flame.

Second, there are feelings of overwhelm. Are you ready to be a parent? Will you be a good dad? Do you have what it takes to care for this little person physically, mentally, emotionally, spiritually, and financially? You may have been grappling with those fears throughout the pregnancy, but when the baby is there, they become very real very fast.

I wish I could tell you these feelings are easy to deal with, but they aren't. In fact, these things, among other causes, can cause both your partner and you to experience mild depression after delivery, which is often called the baby blues.

In this chapter, we'll start by talking about how you can help your wife through the baby blues. We'll also talk about how to identify if this situation grows into something more serious, a condition called postpartum depression (or PPD). Finally, we'll discuss how you can deal with your own negative feelings after delivery.

HOW TO SUPPORT HER THROUGH THE BABY BLUES

After giving birth, it's fairly common for women to experience what's called the baby blues. These blues may include feelings of sadness, anxiety, or overwhelm in the days or weeks after giving birth.

Remember that pregnancy and childbirth are stressful experiences. On top of that, her hormone levels will be on a constant rollercoaster ride. That rollercoaster ride doesn't stop with delivery. Her hormones will continue to fluctuate for months as her body goes through the changes necessary for her to care for a baby, both emotionally and physically.

Do an hour or two of research on the wonders of breastfeeding, on how a mother's milk changes in chemical makeup almost daily to fit the baby's changing nutritional needs. It's amazing, and it helps explain why your partner will continue to undergo crazy (but completely natural) hormonal changes in the months after pregnancy.

While many women report some form of baby blues after childbirth, some continue to suffer from a more severe form of depression called postpartum depression. We'll talk about that in a moment.

Here are a few of the symptoms of the baby blues, completely normal things your wife may experience, especially in the first week after giving birth:

The first week or ten days after having Cody, Linda had just about all of these issues to some degree. I was especially worried about her crying and not being able to sleep. As you probably know, parents get very little sleep the first several weeks after the baby is born anyway, so I really wanted her to take advantage of the times Cody was napping to relax herself. But her blues and anxiety kept her awake.

Thankfully, all of these symptoms started to go away after about a week. And two or three weeks after giving birth, Linda was much more cheerful and calm. Were we still scared stiff about not being able to take care of Cody? Absolutely. But I was happy to see Linda napping with Cody every day, and she seemed to really start connecting with our son in a way that is magical to see.

And that's an important lesson I want you to focus on if you see your wife suffering from one or multiple symptoms listed above: **the baby blues are normal and temporary.** Don't fret about them. Instead, let's talk about some of the things you can do to support your partner through the baby blues.

Be patient with her. Because the baby blues normally last a limited amount of time, don't jump to any conclusions. It's a normal and temporary thing. Be patient with your partner and let her mind and body adjust to the changes.

Be a supportive partner. Do what you can to take things off of your partner's plate, especially the first week after the birth. She's gone through a physically difficult and traumatizing experience. Let her rest up. This will mean doing some extra chores around the house, helping limit how many people (including relatives) come by and visit, and even pulling most of the weight when it comes to taking care of the baby (like diapers and—if you're using formula—middle-of-the-night feeding).

Be positive. Compliment her. Make her feel beautiful and loved. Show her how much you care about the baby. Tell her she's a great mom. Just be generally positive. But, of course, this can backfire if you go overboard. When Linda was feeling down after Cody's birth, I tried being Mister positive. But I did too much too quickly and just ended up irritating her. So be positive, but know when to back off, as well.

As I said above, the baby blues are a temporary condition. Usually, women only experience the above-listed symptoms for a few days. The baby blues may even last for a week or two. What if, however, the symptoms get worse or last even longer? Let's talk about that next.

HOW TO SUPPORT HER THROUGH PPD

If your partner's baby blues get worse or last longer than two weeks, you need to perk up your proverbial ears because a more serious problem may be lurking under the surface. This problem is called postpartum depression, or PPD, and it often is confused with the baby blues at first. How can you tell the difference between the two? Let's look at some of the more serious and longer-lasting symptoms of PPD:

As you can tell from the list, PPD can be a very serious matter. If you and your partner suspect she could be suffering from PPD, you need to reach out to your doctor. Or if the baby blues lasts longer than two weeks, it's best to report it, just to be safe.

If it looks like your wife or partner could be suffering from even a mild form of PPD, as a supportive partner following the Dad Code, you'll have to really step up in taking care of the baby and giving your wife the emotional support she needs.

But what are some specific things you can do? Here are some suggestions:

Address the issue promptly. Don't sink into denial. The longer you fail to address PPD (postpartum depression), the longer the recovery can take. If it seems she is suffering from PPD, schedule an appointment with your doctor as soon as possible.

Show empathy. That means recognizing that she is suffering. Acknowledge that she feels terrible. Also, don't minimize her feelings by telling her that she should just get over it.

Help around the house. If you've been doing this already during the pregnancy because you're supporting her emotionally, then continue with that. Step it up, even. The more you take off her plate, the more she can focus on getting better.

Be a buffer between her and friends and family. Concerned family can be great, and your wife or partner may want to have her mother or another friend or family member with her to help her. But, on the other hand, family and friends can overstay their welcome. They may even make things worse without

114 | CURTIS HOYLES

intending to. So set limits. You have to be your partner's secretary and personal aid. No one gets to see her without going through you first. Relay messages. Answer the phone. Protect your wife from unwanted visitors. (Of course, when visitors are wanted, then you give them access.)

Know your stuff. If PPD is a possible issue in your case, then read up on it. Ask your doctor lots of questions. Sit down with your wife or partner in a quiet setting and write down questions you want to ask a doctor or therapist. Be your wife's medical health advocate by asking the questions she either forgets to ask or doesn't feel up to asking. The more you know, the better you both will be able to recover from this.

Both the baby blues and postpartum depression are challenges that can be overcome. Studies show that women with PPD have a much shorter recovery rate when they have an extremely supportive significant other. So, follow the Dad Code and be there for her during this difficult time.

POSTPARTUM PSYCHOSIS – WHEN TO GET URGENT HELP

Okay, my goal here isn't to scare you. But there is one more level of emotional distress your partner *could* experience. This is very rare, but it's something you need to be on the lookout for. It's called postpartum psychosis. It's the big, scary brother of PPD.

Here are a few symptoms to look out for in your wife or partner:

- Confusion
- Disorientation
- Hallucinations
- Obsessive thoughts about the baby
- Paranoia
- Attempts at self-harm
- Suicide attempt
- Attempts to harm the baby

You don't need me to tell you that these are urgent things that require immediate treatment from a health care professional, right? But I'm going to tell you anyway: if you observe these things, get help immediately.

PPD is fairly rare among women, and postpartum psychosis is extremely rare. But it can lead to life-threatening thoughts or behaviors, so don't delay in seeking medical help. It's what's best for both your partner and your child.

Personally, I know a few people who have dealt with PPD and none who have dealt with postpartum psychosis. But it's always best to be prepared.

We've talked quite a bit about supporting your wife or partner after delivery, but she's not the only one that may experience the blues during those first couple of weeks. You, as the dad, may also go through some depression, anxiety, or feelings of overwhelm. How can you take care of yourself? Let's talk about that next.

THE DADDY BLUES – A REAL THING?

Medical science has been studying the baby blues for a long time. There is a lot of research out there about PPD, as well. But there is an often-overlooked part of parenthood and the days that follow delivery: the "daddy" blues! Yes, fathers can get the baby blues, too.

In fact, some recent studies show that fathers— including adoptive fathers—experience the baby blues and postpartum depression at almost the same rates as women! *How could that be?* You might ask. *After all, the guy isn't going through the same hormonal rollercoaster.*

While it's true that a father isn't on a hormonal roller-coaster during pregnancy, you certainly are on an emotional one. Having a baby is a stressful experience. Even if you adopt a child, you'll experience the same feelings of fear, anxiety, and overwhelm I talked about at the start of this chapter.

Men often feel anxious and displaced for another reason: gender role conflict. In other words, if you were raised in a more "traditional" household, you may have been taught that men go off and work and women stay home and take care of the house. As we've already discussed, you'll have to blur those lines a bit to fully support your wife through pregnancy. That means taking on more cooking and cleaning. It may also mean taking time off from work—at least a week or two. In the US, many companies don't offer much in the way of paternity leave. But if you can take some time off, it's a great idea. But being away from work, cooking, and cleaning all day may be confusing and challenging to your "inner man."

But, hey! Times are changing, and gender roles are shifting, blurring, reversing, or even fading away completely, at least in many aspects of life.

At the same time, if you feel any sort of "daddy blues," you may have to grapple with another additional negative emotion: guilt. That's exactly what happened to me when Liberty was born.

That July Fourth weekend was an unexpected whirlwind of excitement. And while the rest of the world watched the fireworks and drank cheap beers out of aluminum cans—a favorite American pastime—Linda and I were welcoming our second child into the world. It was a beautiful thing. But it was also stressful for me.

You see, we don't exactly make mountains of money with my job. When Cody was born, we had to tighten things down a bit. Linda had been making art pieces and crafts online, selling them on Etsy, and even started making some pretty good extra money before Cody came along. But taking care of him meant Linda had very little time to keep that up, meaning I was the sole breadwinner. But we managed to make things work (with some careful budgeting, of course).

Our second child represented a huge financial struggle for us, and I was really feeling the heat throughout the pregnancy. Knowing we were having a daughter brought on even more anxiety for me. I grew up on Star Wars and Legos and Halo. My little brother and I would play war games with our Nerf guns in the back-yard. We did hard-core boys' stuff. So I kind of felt comfortable being a dad to Cody. But a girl? I had no idea what to do. I felt completely out of my element.

All that anxiety and overwhelm hit me over the next few days after Liberty was born. I'd taken two weeks off from work, and I was careful to give Linda all the support she needed and then some, even though the baby blues were significantly less for her with Liberty than with Cody. All that housework and time away from work made me even more anxious because I just noticed all the little repairs that needed to be done around the house. Everywhere I looked, I saw dollar signs. How was I going to pay for all this?

Then came the *guilt*. Why guilt, you may ask? Well, Linda had good reason to have the baby blues. Pregnancy is a lot of work. Her body had literally just finished growing another human being! Her hormones were all over the place, and she was physically exhausted. Plus, because we decided to breastfeed our children, she had to handle almost all of the feeding duties at first. But what about me? What good reason did I have to feel depressed or overwhelmed?

Add to that the traditional story of the "manly man" that never admits to tender feelings ever, and it's completely understandable that many men who experience any kind of "daddy blues" would keep it to themselves out of guilt and embarrassment. *Just suck it up*, you may be tempted to tell yourself.

But, believe it or not, that is not the right way to handle the "daddy blues." In fact, doing so would be directly in conflict with the Dad Code. How so?

THE DADDY BLUES – HOW TO COPE

If you feel overwhelmed, anxious, or sad after your baby is born—combined with guilt or embarrassment over having such feelings—you'll be tempted to just push them down. And that's understandable. Generations of men in your family probably felt like you do and did exactly that. But is that what's best for you, your partner, or even your baby? What does the Dad Code have to say about it?

Remember the P in P-A-R-R? The P stands for *partner*. It's a reminder that you and your wife are partners in the parenting adventure. You have to be the very best partner you can be so that both of you can provide your child with the best support.

But how can you be a good partner if you hide your feelings from your wife? Good communication is a core aspect of any partnership. And it's also core to a good relationship, which is the first R in P-A-R-R, too.

So, you owe it to your wife to talk about how you feel. In fact, you may have to swallow your pride and seek help outside of the house, as well, like the support of a friend or family member or even a medical professional, such as a psychologist or therapist.

In my case, I turned to my dad for help. I took him out for beers a few days after Liberty was born. I'd already discussed my feelings with Linda, and we both decided it would be best to go to Dad with my problem.

From the start, I had to make it very clear that I wasn't just venting to try and get him to give me money. My dad is nowhere near rich, but I knew he'd generously give the shirt off his back to help my family. I told him I just wanted him to listen. Then I unloaded everything. I told him I was scared and anxious, and overwhelmed. I told him I didn't know how to raise a daughter. I told him the budget would be tighter than ever, and I was scared I'd suddenly lose my job, and we'd end up on the street. I talked about my guilt—about how I didn't feel like it was fair for me to even have these feelings because my whole Dad Code thing was all about me supporting Linda and the children.

And then my dad did the most surprising thing I think I've seen him do in my entire life. He broke down. I mean, tears literally rolled down his red, unshaven cheeks.

I can count on one hand how many times I've seen my dad cry. He's old school like that. He's a tough guy. If we'd grown up in the old west, he'd be the gun-toting sheriff that would gun down every outlaw in the county and ride back home on his manly steed.

And yet he cried with me. He told me he'd felt a lot of those feelings when I was little, especially when my baby brother was born. He told me he had faith in me, that I *would* get through it.

I learned something powerful that day: you're never alone. And you'll never know who else has dealt with the daddy blues unless you speak out about it. Once you break that stigma and traditional expectations of manliness, you'll find out that others have gone through and are going through the same things you are.

And that's the secret to coping!

Seek support. Don't expect too much of yourself all at once. Take things one day at a time. Face the daddy blues together with your partner just like you do her baby blues.

And, if necessary, seek professional help.

Then, before you know it, you'll come out the other side of the daddy blues. Will the anxiety be gone? Nope. Will feelings of overwhelm be a thing of the past? Nuh-uh. Will fatherhood suddenly become a walk in the park? No way!

But you'll come to realize that you *can* do it. With the Dad Code as your guide, you'll learn to tackle any new challenge that comes along.

In fact, starting in the next chapter, we'll talk about some of the biggest challenges of fatherhood, and we'll see how the Dad Code can help you tackle the first several months after delivery with grace, intelligence, and a positive attitude!

REVIEW REQUEST

Enjoyed the Book?

Leave a 1-Click Review!

Reviews are like gold for authors.
Would you please take a few seconds and leave me a
review on Amazon?
I would be super happy.

Scan the QR code below to leave a quick review

7

TENDING TO YOUR NEWBORN'S NEEDS

I was seventeen and scared out of my mind. My grandad was in the passenger seat of my car, an old Buick that had a tendency to just die on the road sometimes. I was pushing the speed limit and barely slowing down for stop signs, praying that I wouldn't cause an accident.

My grandad couldn't breathe. He was wheezing and coughing and shaking all over. I blew through two red lights on the way to the hospital. I knew in that moment if I made one stupid decision—if my car wigged out on me, a cop tried to pull me over, or I hit someone before getting to the hospital, Grandad could die.

I burned rubber as I turned into the hospital parking lot, grateful we'd made it in one piece. My Buick skidded to a stop in front of the double glass doors. I ran inside, yelling, "My grandfather can't breathe. I think he's having a heart attack!"

The receptionist scowled at me. "This is the wrong entrance. The ER is up ahead and around the building."

My face grew hot. "He can't breathe! He's having a heart attack!"

Another nurse appeared out of nowhere with a wheelchair and helped Grandad out of the car. Before I knew it, he was being raced down the hall toward the ER.

Meanwhile, my mind was racing. Did I get there in time? Had I made a big mistake pulling up to the wrong entrance. Would that mistake end up killing him?

Thankfully, he was able to get the help he needed. He's passed now, but he lived more than ten years after that initial heart attack.

But I tell this story to illustrate something important: that day, as I rushed my dying grandfather to the hospital, I felt a terrifying sense of responsibility. It felt like Grandad's life was literally in my hands, and every decision I made felt like life or death.

Before you think I'm just exaggerating here, the cardiologist later told me that if we'd arrived just a couple of minutes later, Grandad wouldn't have made it. His weak heart had caused something called "flash edema," which is when your lungs start to fill with water.

Unless you're an ER doctor, you probably aren't used to making life-and-death decisions on a regular basis. We just aren't used to carrying around that level of responsibility. In fact, in the years that followed, I never had that same weight on my shoulders again. Even at work, since I'm in the human resources department, I know that my work could define who loses their job and who doesn't if the company goes through a hard financial crash. But even that isn't the same as true *life and death*.

Fast-forward to the day Linda and I took our son, Cody, home from the hospital. For the first time since I was seventeen, I was struck by the sudden weight of enormous responsibility. This little person, this tiny, defenseless human being, was our responsibility.

It seems almost comical, doesn't it? You walk into the hospital as a couple. You go through the craziness of labor and delivery, and then you leave as a trio. They just give you this baby and tell you that you have to take care of it from now on!

As a father wanting to follow the Dad Code, you're undoubtedly determined to take that responsibility seriously. So how do you take care of a newborn? What needs does it have? And how can you start early, not just physically providing for it but also start building a powerful father-child relationship? Let's talk about a few essential aspects of infant care, starting with the basics.

HOW TO HANDLE YOUR NEWBORN

A newborn baby may look surprisingly fragile to a new parent. We're used to seeing babies in movies and in public. But a newborn looks distinctly different. Did you know that when newborns are portrayed in most movies, the baby "actor" is actually much older?

So don't be surprised when you see your baby for the first time and they look too weak to do much of anything. They will grow into the classic baby you're used to seeing. In the meantime, you have to handle them with great care.

Always hold your baby by supporting the head and neck. They don't have enough strength in their head muscles to hold their own head up, so you have to do it for them. And, by the way, before you touch your baby, you should wash your hands. This is because newborns have a weak immune system, and you don't want to bombard them with too many germs all at once.

When carrying your newborn, be gentle. Later, there will be plenty of time for "rougher" play, like bouncing them on your knee or throwing them into the air. But those are NOT activities for a newborn. You never, ever shake an infant because it can cause serious and permanent damage.

Finally, when you put your infant into a stroller, car seat, or even in a crib, make sure they are strapped in and secure at all times.

As long as you remember to be gentle, you'll quickly get used to handling your newborn.

DIAPER CHANGING

Ah, the dreaded diapers! Babies poop a lot. You're going to have to get used to that. And, as a follower of the Dad Code, remembering that you are a partner for your wife, you'll be interested in helping out as much as possible with the diaper changing, right?

Newborn poopies are not bad at all. So, it's a great time to get used to the process of changing the diaper. You'll be doing it about ten times a day, after all!

Before you start changing the diaper on your baby, make sure everything you need is within reach. It's a rookie dad mistake to forget the baby wipes or fresh diapers until you're halfway through the process. Then you may have to step away from your baby to grab something, leaving them in a dangerous situation. They could surprise you and try to roll off the changing table, for example. So, think smart and gather your supplies first.

Other than that, changing diapers is fairly easy. You lay the baby on their back, unfasten the diaper and clean them up with a wipe. Be careful about sudden pee attacks. Little boys especially have a tendency to start peeing when they feel the open air down there. It's not just a bit in comedy movies; it really can happen.

When cleaning your baby, remember to be thorough, cleaning the front and back. With girls, you need to wipe from front to back. Otherwise, you may push some of the poop into her vagina, which can cause an infection.

If you're using disposable diapers, these fold up neatly and stay closed because of the tape. With some practice, you'll be able to close diapers in a single, fluid motion. You'll also get better at putting on the new diaper with each changing session. Soon, you'll be the Mr. Miyagi of diaper changing!

Of course, you and your partner may choose to use cloth diapers instead of disposable ones. You may also choose to use washcloths or cotton balls and warm water to clean your baby. Whatever you choose, the basic principles are the same.

FEEDING YOUR BABY – THE PROS AND CONS OF BREASTFEEDING

While your baby was in the womb, they were connected to their mother through the umbilical cord. Through that cord, the unborn child received a constant drip of nutrients from Momma. Once the baby is born, however, they will now have to start feeding in the same way we all do: eating, digesting, and eliminating.

We covered the "eliminating" part in the above section on diaper changing, but now it's time to talk about feeding your baby. And, when it comes to feeding your newborn, you and your wife have an important decision to make: are you going to breastfeed or use formula?

Of course, the decision is completely up to you as a couple, and, ultimately, it's up to the mother how she will feed her baby. Let's look at some pros and cons of breastfeeding, things you may want to think about when making the decision.

Pro: The baby gets health benefits. This is the biggest and most obvious reason why most health organizations support breastfeeding as the best option for the child's health. Earlier in this book, in Chapter 6, I talked briefly about the wonders of breastfeeding, how the mother's milk changes from week to week, acting to boost the baby's immune system and giving them exactly what they need to grow healthily.

Numerous studies over the years have shown that breastfed babies grow faster and stronger. The immune system boost is outstanding, helping to protect babies against ear infections, stomach infections, diarrhea, as well as allergies and asthma. There are also many possible long-term benefits. Some studies show that breastfed babies are less likely to have diabetes later in life, are less likely to be obese as adults, and even have a slight advantage in IQ.

Now, some of these benefits may seem a bit far-fetched. And some studies have been questioned by experts and need more experimentation and review to back them up. Not every breastfeeding benefit you hear about is confirmed by science. But health organizations worldwide agree that breastmilk is the "perfect food" for babies!

Pro: A better connection between mother and child. It's been long documented that babies also get numerous psychological and physical benefits from regular, close human contact. In fact, many of the above-stated benefits to a baby's health and immune system come from—not just the milk itself—but from the skin-to-skin contact a baby gets with Momma while feeding. This also allows the baby and mother to bond on a deeply emotional level.

Pro: Breast milk is free. If you've gone for a little walk through your local grocery store or pharmacy's diaper aisle, you probably came out with a feeling of desperation in the pit of your stomach. Diapers are not cheap, especially when you realize you'll be going through them at a prodigious rate. Well, formula isn't cheap either. Breastfeeding, on the other hand, is completely free. You don't need to buy any special equipment to breastfeed a child. Nature just takes over, and the only financial expense is to ensure your wife eats well.

Pro: The baby is prepared for solid foods. A mother's breast milk comes from the foods she eats. That also means the flavor of the milk will vary slightly depending on what Momma is eating each day. This can be a very good thing. Why? Well, because the baby will get used to the flavors their mother is eating according to her culture and diet. Then, later, when you start adding solid foods to the baby's diet, they may be more open to trying some flavors because they've already been pre-exposed to them early on.

Pro: Mothers benefit, too. There's no doubt that babies benefit from breastfeeding in many ways. But mothers do, too. A mother who breastfeeds her child will bond with them in a deep way because of the regular skin-to-skin contact they have with the child. She may also feel a sense of confidence as a caregiver. The act of breastfeeding changes a mother's body chemistry, burning extra calories and shrinking the uterus. These things may help her get down to her pre-pregnancy weight a bit faster, which can be a huge confidence and self-esteem boost.

Of course, breastfeeding isn't all roses and unicorns. There are some disadvantages to consider, as well. Let's look at some cons to breastfeeding your baby.

Con: It can be uncomfortable (or even painful). When a baby "latches on" to Momma's nipple, this can be a painful experience—especially at first. Some mothers worry that they are doing things wrong because of the pain or discomfort, making the whole experience very stressful. The "latch-on" pain should go away after the first week or so, or you may have to reach out to a lactation consultant or doctor.

Con: It's a huge commitment. Yes, having children in the first place is a huge commitment. But breastfeeding is a whole new level of commitment because it means your wife or partner will have to feed the baby every couple of hours, at least for the first couple of weeks. (We'll get into feeding schedules below.) Of course, the vast majority of this commitment falls on the mother's shoulders, as we'll talk about next.

Con: It all falls on mom. When you formula feed your baby, just about anyone can help out. That means you and your wife can split feeding duties. You can ask a grandparent or nanny to feed the child. Anyone who can properly hold a baby and bottle is up for the challenge. When you commit to breastfeeding, the bulk of the commitment falls on Mom. That means your wife or partner will be up multiple times a night and throughout the day to feed the baby. That will be hard on her, and it will be hard on you, too, because you'll want to help out (as a supportive partner following the Dad Code), but you won't physically be able to.

Con: Loss of autonomy. Women in the modern world have busy professional and social lives. But the commitment behind choosing to breastfeed can interrupt that in a big way. Many women who breastfeed their babies report feelings of being tied to their child.

They may even feel like they've lost ownership of their bodies.

Con: Social pressure or judgment. While medical organizations almost universally support breastfeeding, the general public often has a different opinion. In recent years, breastfeeding has become a political issue, and people may have strong views against breast-feeding or breastfeeding in public. This social pressure may be small but constant.

When Linda was breastfeeding Cody, our first child, she constantly felt out of place in public. Even if she found a quiet place out of public view to feed the baby, and she used a blanket to cover herself, people would often stare in a way that made Linda feel judged or shamed. There was also some negative feedback from Linda's family about her choice. They viewed it as unfair. Some in the family even blamed me, as if I were forcing her to breastfeed instead of it being her choice.

These kinds of social complications aren't really a big deal, but they can be difficult to deal with in the moment. And that social pressure may be enough for a mother to decide not to breastfeed her baby.

Of course, there are tons of potential caveats to several of the above pros and cons. For example, you can store breastmilk in the freezer or fridge (more on that below), so 100% of the responsibility doesn't have to fall on your wife's shoulders. Also, some couples choose a hybrid approach, both breastfeeding and formula feeding their child. That can help in some situations, as well.

As a supportive partner, you want to help your wife make a good decision when it comes to feeding your newborn baby. But, ultimately, the choice is hers because breastfeeding involves her body.

Be prepared for your partner to change her mind, as well. Linda was determined early on in her first pregnancy to breastfeed, but, as the due date approached, she started to consider formula feeding. It wasn't until after Cody was born that she made the final decision. I did some reading, and it turns out this is common.

Your wife or partner may change her mind even after the baby is born, and that's okay. Remember that making the commitment to breastfeed is stressful, and —even if you really want her to make one decision or another—you won't help the situation at all by pressuring her to "stick to her guns" or side with you on the matter. Instead, make it your goal to be supportive and understanding throughout the decision-making process.

Speaking of being supportive, let's look at what you can do as a father to support your partner and your newborn during feeding time, whether you choose to breastfeed, use formula, or a combination of both.

HOW TO SUPPORT HER THROUGH BREASTFEEDING

If your wife or partner decides to breastfeed your baby, commend her on taking on that level of commitment. After all, she is obviously very concerned about putting your baby's health ahead of everything else! How can you support her through the early months of breastfeeding? Here are a few things to consider.

Help her by carrying more of the load. While it's true that breastfeeding means your wife will be taking on the majority of the load when it comes to feeding, you can still do a lot to support her through this process.

First of all, you can take on more than your share of other responsibilities, such as diaper changing and sleep duty. (We'll talk more about sleep in the following chapter.) You can also work to take off as much of a load as you can when it comes to chores around the house. I've already told you that I took up cooking when Linda was pregnant. That carried over to the first few months after Cody was born. In fact, to this day, I handle the majority of dinners. Cooking after work has become a relaxing hobby of mine and a great way to take a huge responsibility off Linda's shoulders.

Who knows? You could one day become an awesome daddy home chef!

Support her emotionally. As a follower of the Dad Code, you've been a great PARTNER by being there for her emotionally throughout the pregnancy and delivery, right? Well, if your wife has chosen to breastfeed, you have an opportunity to keep it up. In fact, you can step up your game by constantly looking for ways to commend and compliment her.

Look for every opportunity to show and tell her you love her. Be supportive. While the baby is feeding, sit with her and have a chat. Listen to her. The more you work out the empathy muscle, the stronger it will get!

Help her with her diet. A breastfeeding woman is basically a natural factory of super nutrient-rich food for her baby. In order to keep that factory strong and effective, her body needs to stay healthy. That means your breastfeeding wife or partner must focus on keeping her diet rich in nutrition. It also means avoiding certain foods or substances.

If it isn't obvious already, smoking is out of the question when it comes to breastfeeding mothers. Other drugs are even more out of the question. The same deadly ingredients in cigarettes or vapes that can hurt Momma will filter down to the baby through the breastmilk. In fact, even if you aren't breastfeeding, being a smoking parent is a very bad idea. Google "third-hand smoking" to find out more, but it's seriously dangerous for babies.

Alcohol is also generally a bad idea. A small percentage of the alcohol a mother drinks will filter down into the baby through the breastmilk, so mothers should either not drink at all or drink very sparingly when breastfeeding. Many medical organizations suggest waiting two hours after having a drink to breastfeed a baby to minimize the amount of alcohol there might be in the milk.

While not everyone agrees on the dangers of caffeine in adults, you may still want to limit your wife's caffeine intake while breastfeeding. This is because some of that caffeine will filter down to the baby, making them hyper or irritable. A cup or two of coffee is fine, but she should avoid heavy caffeine use since it will only result in the baby keeping both of you up all night.

HOW TO STORE BREASTMILK

While it's true that the majority of the load of breast-feeding falls on the mother, it isn't necessarily true that she becomes the only person that can *ever* feed your newborn. Breastmilk can be stored, reheated, and safely given to babies, meaning you can feed the baby between "authentic" breastfeeding sessions, giving Momma a much-needed break.

You can buy an apparatus that will gently suck a small amount of breastmilk from your wife or partner's breasts and store it in a small bottle. You can then store this milk in the fridge or freezer for short periods of time. There are generally three ways to store breastmilk:

- At room temperature, in an airtight bottle. (Only up to 4 hours.)
- In the back of the refrigerator. (Up to 4 days.)
- In the back of the freezer. (Up to 6 months.)

Notice that I suggest putting the milk in the *back* of the fridge or freezer. This is because the front of the fridge varies greatly in temperature based on how often you open the door.

Be very careful about storing breastmilk. The nutrients can degrade over time, and—even worse—you run the risk of giving the baby an infection. I've personally never let breastmilk sit out longer than 3 hours in a cool room, and we'd only keep breastmilk in the back of the fridge until the next day, just to be safe.

Also, you should never thaw or warm up milk in the microwave. This is for two reasons. First, you can easily overheat it, and that would burn the baby's little mouth or throat. Second, microwaving can degrade the nutrients, defeating the purpose of using breastmilk in the first place.

Instead of nuking the milk, heat it up slowly in a pot of water on the stove. You don't want the milk to be hot to the touch. In fact, it should barely be warm. Put the end of your finger in your mouth. Feel the slight warmth of your body temperature? You want the milk to be the same temp.

Thanks to storing breastmilk, I was able to give Linda nights or days off from the load of breastfeeding. That way, she could catch up on sleep, make plans to go out and have lunch with friends, or just go shopping for a couple of hours without having to lug the baby around.

THE HYBRID APPROACH

Another option for some families is a hybrid approach. You can try breastfeeding and formula feeding your baby. The drawback to this is that babies will sometimes decide they don't like to combo and start rejecting either the breastmilk or the formula.

It's kind of like having your favorite pair of jeans. I often like to buy multiple pairs of the same jeans whenever I need to. If one pair is different from the others, I'll end up having a favorite. And, once I have a favorite, I'll avoid wearing the jeans I don't like as much.

Well, babies might do the same with formula vs. breastfeeding. So it's often best to stick to one or the other. Storing breastmilk is a great way to free up Momma without having to add formula.

FORMULA FEEDING YOUR BABY

There are many reasons why a couple may opt to formula feed their baby. Some women may have a medical condition that knocks breastfeeding out as an option. Or career commitments may require your partner to leave the home for multiple hours a day, meaning formula feeding (or storing breast milk) is the best option.

Whatever the reasons for choosing to formula feed your baby, here are some key principles to follow when it comes to formula feeding.

Not all formulas are created equal. When choosing the best formula for your baby, do your research. Just going with the cheapest option may not be the best idea. On the other hand, many companies make "luxury" or "premium" formulas with little to no real benefits that justify the price tag.

Buy age-appropriate formula. We haven't talked a lot about the A in P-A-R-R in this book. Don't worry; the A comes in very handy later in your child's life. But this is one case where being age-appropriate is very important. Babies need different nutrients based on their age. So don't give your baby formula from the wrong age group.

Budget formula expenses. By some estimates, parents will spend nearly two thousand dollars on baby formula per child. This is an expense you'll want to save for and have at the top of your budget.

Prepare for the future. Make sure you have a safe stock of formula at home at all times. The last thing you want is to have a crying, hungry baby in your arms, only to find out you're out of formula! Also, supply chain issues and health-related recalls can suddenly affect how much formula is in your local grocery store or pharmacy—so have extra at home at all times.

THE IDEAL FEEDING SCHEDULE

Some people will tell you to set a schedule for feeding your baby. A quick Google search will reveal all kinds of timetables and schedules, such as every two hours, every three hours, or even every thirty minutes! But don't be fooled by such schedules.

A newborn baby will generally need to eat every two to three hours. Many trusted medical organizations will tell you that the best schedule for feeding your baby is demand-based. That means you feed your baby when they let you know they are hungry.

As I mentioned above, a newborn's stomach is about the size of a marble when they are born. That means they can't hold a lot of food at any one time. It also means they will be hungry often. Forcing a hungry baby to wait to eat will only harm their natural growth and immune systems. It's best to learn to identify when the baby is hungry and provide food on demand.

WHEN TO INTRODUCE SOLID FOOD

This book deals primarily with the periods of your wife's pregnancy and delivery, as well as the first couple of weeks of your baby's life. During that time, you shouldn't even think about adding solid food to their diet. Many medical organizations suggest waiting at least four months before adding any kinds of solids.

In addition to that, you don't want to give the baby any fluid that isn't breastmilk or formula. That includes water, juice, or cow's milk.

Another thing you must avoid for the entire first year of the baby's life is honey. Honey has many powerful health benefits for adults, but it can be harmful to babies.

All in all, when your baby is a newborn, just stick to either breastmilk or formula. Feed the baby whenever it is hungry and allow the miracle of nature to take its wonderful course. When it comes to taking care of your baby, however, there is one major area of concern you have to think about, and that is sleeping. Sleep is such a major topic that I decided to give it a chapter on its own.

8

PUTTING YOUR NEWBORN TO
SLEEP

There is this scene in Star Wars: Empire Strikes Back where Luke Skywalker, while training on the jungle planet Dagobah with Master Yoda, encounters a cave full of the Dark Side of the Force. Luke has an eerie feeling the second he sees this cave, and, when he goes inside, he encounters his greatest fear: Darth Vader.

As you take your newborn baby home from the hospital, you may have a similar feeling to Luke. The dark cave you face now isn't full of the Dark Side of the Force. There is no Sith lord with a lightsaber waiting for you inside. Instead, what awaits you is far more challenging: sleepless nights!

It's no secret that new parents are sleep deprived. I wish there were a way for me to sugarcoat this for you, but there isn't. Newborn babies sleep a lot—like between 14 and 17 hours in any 24-hour period. But they don't have a regular sleep schedule. They'll wake up and cry every 2 or 3 hours to feed. They'll cry when they have a dirty diaper. They'll cry when they want to be held. They'll cry for no apparent reason at all.

Baby cries will pull you out of sleep more times than you can count in the first few months of your child's life. This is a fact of nature. That being said, there are things you can do to help your baby sleep better. There are also some tips and tricks I've picked up to help first-time fathers deal with sleep deprivation and inter-rupted nights.

ADJUST YOUR EXPECTATIONS

I've always been a pretty goal-driven guy. I'm good at what I do at work, I have a regular fitness routine, and I've always had the dream of becoming a full-time writer. I always have ambitious goals written in my bullet journal, and I have to stay organized to accomplish everything I want to do each week.

If you're also driven, you may have this idea that, within a week or two of your baby's birth, you'll be able to get back on track with your ambitions. As the due date approaches, you may dream of getting back into your workout routine and jumpstarting that side hustle you've been thinking about throughout the pregnancy.

Well, let me tell you this now, so you're not even more disappointed later: life *won't* return to normal right after delivery. The sleepless nights will take their toll. And the very best thing you can do is expect less from yourself for the first few months after your baby is born.

I'm not saying you shouldn't have any goals at all. But you'll need to be there for your wife or partner, and you'll be spending a lot of time bonding with your baby. (More on bonding in the following chapter.)

So the first way to overcome sleepless nights is to adjust your expectations. Put those major fitness or career goals off by a few more months and focus on getting fatherhood right from day one.

HOW TO PROTECT YOUR BABY FROM SIDS

For the first few months of your baby's life, getting your baby to sleep shouldn't be a problem at all. This is because a healthy, growing baby will naturally sleep most of the time, even though they wake up regularly, too. During this early time, your biggest focus should be on making sure your baby sleeps safely. Why is safety an issue?

You've probably heard of SIDS, which stands for *sudden infant death syndrome.* I know that sounds crazy scary, but it is an incredibly rare thing that happens. Babies can sometimes die in their sleep, which is why SIDS is sometimes known as *crib death.* While SIDS is not completely understood, there are things you can do to *significantly reduce the risk* of it happening in your baby's case. First, here are a few non-sleep-related things you can do to reduce the risk of SIDS:

Don't smoke. I know we've talked about the dangers of smoking a lot in this book already, but studies show that second-hand smoke increases the risk of SIDS.

Breastfeed. We talked about the pros and cons of breastfeeding in the previous chapter. While the decision to breastfeed is a personal one, it's good to know that breastfed babies are less likely to have SIDS.

Help Momma be nourished and healthy. Well-nourished and healthy mothers have babies who are less likely to die in the crib. So go back and look at the early chapters on health and exercise to help your wife or partner be as healthy as possible through the pregnancy.

With these three factors in place, you already make your baby much less at risk of SIDS. But, as we'll see in the following section, there are things you can do when putting your baby to sleep to make it much less at risk.

HOW TO PUT YOUR BABY TO SLEEP SAFELY

Even healthy infants can suffer from SIDS, but many factors in how the baby sleeps affect the risk of SIDS. Here are some things you can do to ensure your baby is sleeping safely.

Sleep in the same room. Babies that sleep in the same room as their parents for the first six months are at a much lower risk of SIDS.

But not in the same bed. That said, a baby that sleeps in the bed with Momma is more likely to die in their sleep. So get a crib and keep it near the bed instead.

Keep a comfortable temperature. A comfortable and cool temperature is best for helping the baby to sleep soundly and not stop breathing in their sleep. The risk of SIDS increases if the baby is hot in their sleep.

Sleep the baby on its back. Babies that sleep on their stomachs or side are at a higher risk of SIDS.

Sleep them on a cleared, firm mattress. Babies should not sleep on overly soft surfaces. A firm mattress with a tight-fitting sheet is best. And keep pillows, blankets, and stuffed animals away from the baby while it sleeps.

Make sure the baby can move freely. Babies wrapped up tight in a blanket are more likely to have trouble breathing, leading to SIDS. So keep them in a onesie that allows them to move their arms and legs regularly.

HOW TO ESTABLISH A CIRCADIAN RHYTHM

A circadian rhythm is your body's internal clock when it comes to going to sleep and waking up. Over time, we naturally establish a rhythm, waking up at about the same time every day and going to sleep at the same time every night. Over time, you want to help your child establish a similar rhythm, so they are used to napping at the same time every day, going to bed, and staying asleep throughout the night.

Of course, you can't expect a newborn to do any of these things. Their rhythm is going to be erratic. That's natural and healthy. But there are things you can do to help your baby start developing a circadian rhythm as early as possible.

Use natural daylight in the home. As much as possible, open the windows and fill your home with natural daylight during the day. Daylight has a powerful effect on our brains, helping to establish our own sleep rhythms.

Keep the home dimly lit at night. On the flip side, don't use harsh lights during the night. Soft, dim, warm lights (without blue light) will tell both you and the baby's brain that it's still night and time to go back to sleep.

Establish a sleepy time routine. Many parents have great bedtime routines with their kids. For example, I've read to Cody almost every night of his life. Bedtime stories are a huge part of our life and something everyone in the family cherishes. Establish a bedtime routine with your infant from the start, with stories, calming music, or even a baby massage. Over time, this will signal to the baby that it's time to go to sleep.

Again, keep in mind that your baby won't have anything close to a recurring sleep schedule for several months. That is completely normal. But the earlier you start helping your baby establish a circadian rhythm, the sooner you'll go back to having full nights of sleep yourself!

HOW TO TAKE CARE OF YOUR SLEEP

Speaking of your sleep, you and your partner need to do your utmost to get enough sleep during these early months. How can you do that? By following some common sleep best practices, such as the following:

Get outside every day. It may seem counterintuitive, but natural sunlight is vital to your quality of sleep. As I mentioned above, you should allow as much natural sunlight into your home as possible during the day, but you should also get outside. Let the sun warm your skin. Breathe the fresh air. Take advantage of every opportunity to commune with nature, even if you live in the middle of a major city. These things aren't just for tree-hugging hippies! Study after study has shown that getting into nature and exposure to sunlight improves your sleep.

Limit bright lights, blue light, and screen time before bed. As already said about improving your baby's sleep, you should avoid harsh lights, especially blue light, before sleep. You should also limit screen time. A soothing nighttime atmosphere will help you sleep better and get back to sleep faster after the baby has woken you up for the third time in any given night.

Limit caffeine, sugar, and alcohol. Caffeine is obviously the enemy of sleep. Many adults limit or cut out caffeine completely, especially in the afternoons. You should consider doing the same, at least for the first six months of your baby's life, since this will help both of you get to sleep faster when the baby is asleep. Many studies show that refined sugars and alcohol also diminish the quality of our sleep, so cut those down to a minimum during this time.

Divide nighttime duties fairly. As a father who's following the Dad Code, you want to be a good *partner*, and that means wanting to take your share of nighttime interruptions so your wife or partner can get back to sleep. Even if the baby is breastfeeding, can you store a few ounces of breastmilk each night so you can feed the baby at least once per night, allowing your wife to just turn over and get some extra sleep?

By not putting too much pressure on yourself during the first few months, putting the baby to sleep in a safe way and doing what you can to take care of both the baby's and your circadian rhythms, you'll be able to make the most of this challenging and sleepless time of your lives. Before you know it, your baby will get older and start sleeping most or all of the night! Then, much like Luke Skywalker, you'll feel an awful lot like a Jedi!

9

BALANCING TWO VITAL RELATIONSHIPS

There is nothing better than holding your newborn baby in your arms.

I remember carrying Cody around the house that first week, gently humming to him while Linda tried to catch up on sleep. Babies are fun to watch, even when they're asleep, because they often make noises, move their little hands, and even kick while sound asleep. This is because their little bodies, brains, and nervous systems are actively growing every minute of the day. Sometimes, they even wake themselves up because of their own movements, and the startled little face they make is priceless.

It's hard to describe my emotional state those first couple of weeks. Linda and I were both exhausted, and little Cody kept waking us up at all hours of the night. Yet, at the same time, I couldn't have been happier. My heart leaped every time I saw him—*my son*—and I wanted to provide for him and protect him with every fiber of my being.

More than that, now that he was *here*, a little human being instead of just the idea of a baby growing inside of my wife's womb, I was more determined than ever to be a good dad. And that meant really connecting with my boy.

Up to this point, we've focused only on the first of the two R's in P-A-R-R—the Dad Code. Both R's stand for the same thing: *relationship*. The R is repeated to remind you that, once your child is born, you will now have two relationships you'll value more than anything else in the universe—your ongoing friendship and romantic relationship with your wife or partner and the brand-new relationship you'll have with your child.

Those two R's are completely separate because, for the most part, each relationship will require effort from you to build and maintain. It's kind of like trying to keep two plates spinning simultaneously, which means it requires a good deal of balance.

So, in this final chapter, I want to discuss this balancing act. First, let's talk about how you can start growing your father-child relationship from the first couple of days your baby is in your home. Then, we'll talk about how you can weather the challenges of a continuing mommy-daddy relationship. Finally, we'll talk about how you can balance these two Rs in a positive and sustainable way.

THE FIRST R – BONDING WITH YOUR BABY

Look up "bonding with your baby" on Google, and almost all of the tips will be specifically about mothers bonding with their children. Once again, fathers are kind of left out. And, while it's completely true that mothers absolutely must bond with their babies early on, it's completely false to think that dads have to wait until some future time to start connecting with their babies.

In fact, I strongly believe that the first week is the best time for the father to start bonding with his baby. You want to be a supportive father, after all, right? And that means you'll want to share parenting responsibilities and give your wife or partner some much-needed time off. So, while you're changing diapers, feeding, or simply holding and comforting your baby, you can also use that time to plant the seeds for a life-long positive father-child relationship.

But how can you bond with your baby? Here are some tips I've found useful.

Make eye contact and smile. This is simple. In fact, it may seem too simple, but it's a powerful way to start bonding with your child. Humans, like many animals, are hard-wired to recognize eye contact. Even newborns with blurry vision can tell when someone is looking at them, and you'll see your baby looking—not just seeing, but actively looking—back at you. Now, if you smile warmly, you'll start building a strong connection immediately. Newborns are also hard-wired to recognize a smile!

Talk in soothing tones. Babies also recognize the tone of your voice from day one. That means that when you speak to your baby in a peaceful and soothing tone, you put your baby at ease and make them more comfortable around you.

Give lots of physical contact, even skin to skin. Breastfeeding mothers get to give lots of skin-to-skin contact to their babies, and this triggers massive changes in the body chemistry of both the baby and the mother. But that effect isn't limited to women. You can bond with your baby on a deeply emotional level when you give skin-to-skin contact. Allow the baby to feel your warmth and feel comforted and protected in your arms or on your chest.

Stroke, soothe, and massage your baby. Babies respond to touch more than any other sense in those early days. You can use this to your advantage by massaging, soothing, and cuddling your child. Remember to be gentle, though! One day you'll be able to rough-house with your child, but not when they're a newborn!

Of course, the one thing that underlies every one of these tips is simply spending time with your child. Even when your wife or partner is holding or taking care of the baby, you can still be there. The baby should quickly get used to your presence, your voice and face. The more time you spend, the better.

THE SECOND R – MANAGING A CHANGING ROMANTIC RELATIONSHIP

While having a baby is both exciting and tiring, and you'll be very interested in bonding with your child, you'll also quickly realize that your relationship with your wife or partner is also going through some changes.

For one thing, your lives will suddenly be structured almost completely around the baby, especially in those first couple of months when the baby is waking up constantly and demanding attention. But the level of distraction goes beyond that because the lack of sleep will wear on both of your nerves, meaning you'll be less patient than you used to be. This can lead to arguments over the dumbest of issues.

Because of these challenges and changes, you may start to feel like your relationship is in danger. And, as a follower of the Dad Code, you'll still want to pay lots of attention to that first R and maintain your relationship with your wife or partner. How can you do that?

Be patient. As I said in the last chapter about your goals and ambitions in life, realize that patience is needed when dealing with relationship issues. Linda and I have always had a "don't go to sleep while angry" policy, which has kept our relationship strong. Yet, when sleep is at a premium, we had to realize that putting some minor issues on hold and giving some time to the baby isn't a bad thing. If or when you start to feel frustrated about your relationship with your significant other, or when you fight about something you never fought about before, don't lose hope. Just remember: *this too shall pass.*

Talk things out. While patience is important, don't leave too many things to fester when you and your wife can still talk things out. Learn to be very clear with your communication.

A lot of your conversations may start to feel like business negotiations as you divvy up diaper changes, nights off, and feeding times. But that's totally okay. Be very clear about what you need and show that you're willing to help in giving her what she needs, too.

Revive your romantic streak. Sincerely compliment her on every occasion you can. Take ten minutes to write her a love note. Buy her some flowers when you go out for diapers or formula. These little things make a big difference, reminding her that you still care and love her. At the same time, if she goes the extra mile to make a romantic gesture to you, show your appreciation wholeheartedly. Romance, like a campfire, must be fed regularly to stay bright and hot.

Schedule couple time. Let's put it plainly—after a baby is born, there is less sex. Aside from that, there is less time for dates, romantic dinners, or movie nights. But you can show your wife or partner that couple time is important to you by making the needed arrangements. Sure, romance—and sexy time—may feel strange if it's penciled into a calendar instead of spontaneous. But you'll be surprised how easy it is to get used to "scheduled romance." In fact, you'll find out you enjoy that time immensely because you'll be looking forward to it ahead of time!

HOW TO BALANCE THE TWO R'S

I wish I could tell you it's easy, but it isn't. Finding the right balance is only something you can do together— as mother and father. But if you openly communicate your needs and feelings, you'll be able to work together to make sure both your relationships as parents and a couple continue to grow.

As part of that balancing act, you can sometimes find ingenious solutions to multiple problems. Let me give you an example.

After Cody was born, since Linda and I lived in the same town as my parents, we had the problem of some overwhelming grandparents. My mom was coming over almost every day, and my dad—a bit surprisingly, I'll admit—was almost as bad. They were becoming overbearing and driving a still sleep-deprived Linda a little bit crazy.

I'd started back at work at the time and was also sleep deprived. Since I was trying to support Linda as much as possible in the evenings and through the night, I was getting very little sleep and then working all day. On top of that, Linda and I were quickly becoming strangers. We were almost never awake at the same time. We were passing Cody back and forth like runners in a relay race.

Finally, Linda and I sat down to discuss these challenges, and the solution was staring us right in the face. We could use one problem (the overbearing grandparents) as the solution for another (sleep deprivation and lack of couple time). So, we prepared ourselves thoroughly and sat my parents down for a little chat.

We thanked them for their constant help and support in these first several weeks of Cody's life. But we also tactfully asked them if we could better structure the help they were offering instead of them popping over randomly. My parents were eager to help.

As a result, we were able to organize things so that my parents could watch Cody on predetermined nights so that Linda and I could go on dates. We'd walk around a local park, go to a movie, or go out to eat. On a couple of occasions, we saved up enough money to reserve a night at a local hotel. While my parents might have imagined a night full of what my mom calls "honeymooning," we actually spent most of these nights sleeping like the dead!

Using my parents in this way also limited the number of unplanned "pop-ins," allowing Linda and I to spend plenty of family time with Cody, too. We got used to watching movies at low or no volume, just reading the subtitles, while we cuddled together with the baby.

As a result of our little plan, I felt like I was better able to bond with Cody without my mom barging in to take him away from me. At the same time, Linda and I were able to regularly schedule couple time, which helped our relationship completely.

Now, I know your specific challenges may not be the same as mine. The plan to use the grandparents to make time as a couple may not apply to your situation. But it illustrates what you can accomplish when you talk things out and express your challenges, needs, and expectations as a couple.

Really, the issue of balancing the two R's only becomes a problem when you don't recognize and address it. When you realize that both of those R's should be important to you, you'll easily be able to work with your wife or partner on a solution that meets everyone's needs!

REVIEW REQUEST

Enjoyed the Book?

Leave a 1-Click Review!

Reviews are like gold for authors.
Would you please take a few seconds and leave me a
review on Amazon?
I would be super happy.

Scan the QR code below to leave a quick review

CONCLUSION

Books, courses, and classes on pregnancy and taking care of a baby are all too often focused almost completely on the mother. This is understandable because the mother is the one that carries the baby to term and—traditionally—takes the lead in caring for the child. But where's the father in all of this?

Dads are usually left out of the conversation, and I think this is really sad. After all, while Mother Nature made sure a woman can have a baby and take care of it on her own if need be, mothers are universally more successful when they have a reliable and caring support system. And, as the father, you are in the perfect position to be a major component of that support system.

In this book, we've focused mostly on two of the four letters in the Dad Code—P-A-R-R. We've discussed the P, which stands for *partner*, and we've talked a lot about the first of the two R's, which represents your *relationship* with your wife or partner.

Yes, fathers can and should be active and supportive partners to their wives. We've seen how you can be a good partner every step of the way throughout the pregnancy, delivery, and beyond. We've also seen how you can build, strengthen, and maintain a strong relationship with your wife or partner throughout the pregnancy. This relationship will be the backbone of your growing family!

Of course, you can do so much more and holding your newborn in your arms is only the climax of the first chapter of your life as a father.

What can you do to make a success of the information presented in this book?

TURN KNOWLEDGE INTO ACTION

Maybe you picked up this book the day you found out your wife or partner was pregnant. Or maybe you started reading it at some point in the pregnancy. Either way, you still have time to turn the information I've presented to you into action.

Nothing I've told you in this book does you (or your wife or child) any good unless you put it into practice. So take action! Don't let this book collect dust (even digital dust) on a shelf. Instead, turn the Dad Code into a way of life by taking action.

CONTINUE YOUR FATHERHOOD JOURNEY

This book focuses almost completely on pregnancy and delivery, with a few helpful tips you can apply in the first few weeks of your baby's life. But there is so much more to learn! I hope this time we've spent together is only the start of a beautiful partnership. And I hope you're excited to continue learning about the Dad Code and how to put it into action!

LET'S TAKE THIS JOURNEY TOGETHER!

In the Spring of 2022, with both of my children finally in school and the COVID-19 pandemic finally cooling off a bit, I found myself with a bit more time on my hands. As I've mentioned in this book, I've had a life-long dream of becoming an author. I always thought I'd be the next George Lucas and write the Star Wars of a new generation.

But, after reflecting on the challenges of fatherhood and all the things I've learned along the way, I decided to funnel all the skills and practice I've had in writing to create not a space opera novel but a book on the Dad Code. The result was the book you've just read.

As I started writing this book, though, it became immediately apparent to me that I didn't just want to publish a helpful how-to and move on. Over the past decade of fatherhood, I've become increasingly passionate about the Dad Code, and I'm increasingly driven to help fathers like you make a success of being a dad. That means much more than just writing one book.

So I've made my decision: I'll be writing more books, and I'll be looking for more ways to help first-time dads overcome the challenges of raising a kid in this crazy world we all share.

That means I want you to become more than a reader. I want us to be partners. Let's embark on the journey of fatherhood together!

A FREE SURPRISE GIFT JUST FOR YOU!

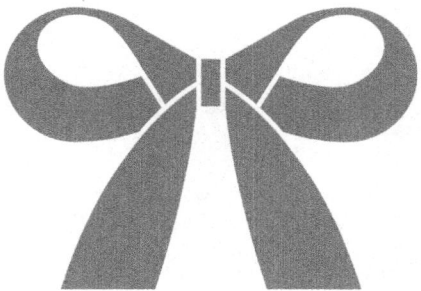

Thank you for purchasing my book.

For all my readers, I have a special thank-you gift that you can access by scanning the QR code below!

BIBLIOGRAPHY AND FURTHER READING

5 Ways to Keep Your Relationship Strong After Having a Baby. (2015, October 20). Psychology Today. https://www.psychologytoday. com/intl/blog/women-s-mental-health-matters/201510/5-ways-keep-your-relationship-strong-after-having-baby

7 Marriage Issues You'll Face After Baby and How to Solve Them. (2021, November 16). Parents. https://www.parents.com/parenting/rela tionships/staying-close/marriage-after-baby/

12 Tips to Help You Prepare for Childbirth and Labor. (2015, June 11). Parents. https://www.parents.com/pregnancy/giving-birth/labor-and-delivery/8-steps-to-a-less-stressful-labor/

15 Great Ways To Support Her During Pregnancy. (2022, May 23). Belly-Belly. https://www.bellybelly.com.au/men/15-great-ways-to-support-your-partner-during-pregnancy/

Bhatia, A. (2016, May 25). *What To Expect When Your Wife Is Expecting.* Babygaga. https://www.babygaga.com/what-to-expect-when-your-wife-is-expecting/

C, T. (2020, October 21). *How Can Husband Help or Support During Labour?* FirstCry Parenting. https://parenting.firstcry.com/articles/how-can-husband-help-or-support-during-labour/

Christiano, D. (2019, August 28). *Baby Feeding Schedule: A Guide to the First Year.* Healthline. https://www.healthline.com/health/parent ing/baby-feeding-schedule

Colleen de Bellefonds, Contributing Editor/Writer. (2022, May 26). *The Best Pregnancy Workouts and Exercises You Can Do While Expecting.* What to Expect. https://www.whattoexpect.com/preg nancy/exercises-for-pregnant-women

Dads: preparing for relationship changes after baby. (2018, July 10). Raising Children Network. https://raisingchildren.net.au/pregnancy/dads-guide-to-pregnancy/early-pregnancy/dads-relationship-changes

Diet Guidelines: 0–12 Months. (2017, August 17). OnHealth. https://www.onhealth.com/content/1/diet_guidelines_0-12_months

Exercising During Pregnancy. (2006, December 1). WebMD. https://www.webmd.com/baby/guide/exercise-during-pregnancy

For Dads: What To Do, What Not To Do When Your Wife Has PPD. (2011, March 20). Psychology Today. https://www.psychologytoday.com/us/blog/isnt-what-i-expected/201103/dads-what-do-what-not-do-when-your-wife-has-ppd

A Guide for First-Time Parents (for Parents) - Nemours KidsHealth. (2018, January). Kids Health. https://kidshealth.org/en/parents/guide-parents.html

Harvey, A., Taylor, A. P., & Nierenberg, C. (2022, January 19). *Signs of labor: 6 clues baby is coming soon.* Livescience.Com. https://www.livescience.com/44554-signs-of-labor.html

How to Talk to Your Baby. (2016, April 27). WebMD. https://www.webmd.com/parenting/baby/baby-talk-language

Infant Sleep (0 to 12 months). (n.d.). KFL&A Public Health. https://www.kflaph.ca/en/healthy-living/Sleep.aspx

Is There (a Sex) Life After Birth? 10 Ways to Bring Back That Lovin' Feeling. (n.d.). ParentMap. https://www.parentmap.com/article/is-there-a-sex-life-after-birth-10-ways-to-bring-back-that-lovin-feeling

Medical Care During Pregnancy (for Parents) - Nemours KidsHealth. (2022, February). Kids Health. https://kidshealth.org/en/parents/medical-care-pregnancy.html

Parent-child Bonding Ideas at Every Age. (n.d.). Babycenter.Com. https://www.babycenter.com/baby/behavior/parent-child-bonding-ideas-at-every-age_10414672

Postpartum depression - Symptoms and causes. (2022, May 24). Mayo Clinic. https://www.mayoclinic.org/diseases-conditions/postpartum-depression/symptoms-causes/syc-20376617

Sudden infant death syndrome (SIDS) - Symptoms and causes. (2022, May 20). Mayo Clinic. https://www.mayoclinic.org/diseases-conditions/sudden-infant-death-syndrome/symptoms-causes/syc-20352800

Taylor, B. (2017, February 23). *Going back to work: A new dad survival guide*. Direct Advice for Dads. https://directadvicefordads.com.au/ new-dads/going-back-to-work-a-new-dad-survival-guide/

Top Ten Terms & Definitions For All Expecting Dads. (2022, February 18). Daddy's Digest. https://daddysdigest.com/top-ten-terms-defini tions-for-all-expecting-dads/

Worksheets/Strategies: Parents workload with a new baby. (n.d.). What Were We Thinking! https://www.whatwerewethinking.org.au/parents/ parents-workload#.Yr4h2BXMK3B

Printed in Great Britain
by Amazon

16639048R00102